Theology
for
Atheists

"It would be hard to imagine a more moral town than Dayton. The relatively wicked, when they would indulge themselves, go to Robinson's Drug Store and debate theology."

H. L. Mencken — *The Scopes Trial*

"Without religion modern man goes crazy."

C.G.Jung — *letters*

Theology for Atheists

GERALD ROBINSON

WIPF & STOCK · Eugene, Oregon

Wipf and Stock Publishers
199 W 8th Ave, Suite 3
Eugene, OR 97401

Theology for Atheists
By Robinson, Gerald
Copyright©2016 by Robinson, Gerald
ISBN 13: 978-1-5326-8040-3
Publication date 2/21/2019
Previously published by Nisbet House, 2016

The Large Hadron Collider image (Fig. 5) courtesy of CERN, Geneva, Switzerland. Shiva Nataraja image (Fig. 6) courtesy of the Cleveland Museum of Art / the Wade Collection. All other illustrations by the author.

CONTENTS

CHAPTER ONE: page 1. *Can Atheists have a Theology?*
Science and Doubt, The Pascal Conspiracy, Celestial Life Insurance.

CHAPTER TWO: page 13. *Do Atheists have Souls?*
A Universal Consciousness. The New Thought Movement.

CHAPTER THREE: page 27. *Faith or Reason?*
Choosing What Is True. Knowing and/or Believing.

CHAPTER FOUR: page 39 *Three Cosmic FAQ's*
Where Do We Come From? Creating the Creator

CHAPTER FIVE: page 61 *Why Are We Here?*
Happy Accident or Intelligent Design? Design Unpacked, Winding Paley's Watch.

CHAPTER SIX: page 83 *Where are we going?*
Great Heavens Above; Catholic, Jehovah, Anglican, Salvationist, Jewish, Muslim, Masonic, and Pets' Heavens. Ultimate Choice.

CHAPTER SEVEN: page 95 *Heavenly Warfare*
Atheist Anger Management.

CHAPTER EIGHT: page 105 *Forging the Divinity of Jesus*
Promoting Jesus, Divine Multiplication, Triangulating the Square, Imagining God.

CHAPTER NINE: page 121 *Following the Secular Jesus*
Jesus as Teacher, Jesus as Leader, Jesus as Priest, Jesus Reproaches, Jesus Redux.

CHAPTER TEN: page 131 *What Earthly Use Is Religion?*
I Believe… , Doing Good, Christian Atheists, Atheists in Christian Communities.

CHAPTER ELEVEN: page 151 *Agony of the Agnostics*
Russell's Teapot, Schrödinger's Pets, Agnostic Agonies.

CHAPTER TWELVE: page 159 *Can Atheists save the Church?*

CHAPTER THIRTEEN: page 167 *The Thirteenth Guest*

CHAPTER ONE

Can Atheists have a Theology?

THEOLOGY is the study of concepts of God and of the nature of religious truths.

People of faith believe that ATHEISTS do not believe in God.

ATHEISTS believe that there is no God. They see no proof or evidence for the existence of God, and up to now people of faith have not been able to furnish any. From this, Atheists assert that the existence of the known universe and everything in it is consistent with the non-existence of God.

THEOLOGY FOR ATHEISTS is the study of concepts for non-existent Gods, and of truths that are not true. It embraces serious frivolity. Typically frivolous is the medieval question "How many angels can dance on the head of a pin?". A more serious question would be "What is the pin pushed into? And who pushed it?". THEOLOGY FOR ATHEISTS examines what does not exist. It is the study of nothing. But to quote John Lennon in Strawberry Fields "Nothing is Real" . . . it really is!

In mathematics nothing is indicated by zero, the most beautiful of all the mathematical symbols—a circular line forming a boundary between an empty space and the rest of our space that is full of stuff: oxygen, armchairs, temples and teapots. That boundary preserves our existence from non-existence. The empty space indicated by zero may also serve as a placeholder in numerical arrays, shifting digits to convert seven to seventy while adding nothing.

Zero is where positive meets negative, an OFF that enables all ON's, one half of a binary which forms the basis of all computer codes. A universal state of "OFF" modulates the "ON" states of all the individual toasters in creation. Is the "OFF" of a toaster different from the "OFF" on a stereo? Certainly. The one delivers silence and the other delivers breakfast, so it follows that there can be many different non-existent realities; many different sorts of non-existent Gods. This provides an atheist answer to an ancient question: if the angels created by a non-existent God are also non-existent, then each one occupies zero space and there would be room for an infinite number of them to cha cha cha on the head of a pin.

Science and Doubt

Science is the field of study which has the most stringent requirements for precise and logical thought, so it is hardly surprising that most scientists are atheists. Recent studies reveal that only 7 per cent of members of the American National Academy of Sciences admit to a belief in God, and for members of the UK's Royal Society only 3.3 per cent believe in God. This indicates that the vast majority, over 90 percent of scientists are doubters. They are trained to this. Doubt is what lies at the heart of the scientific method.

A rigorous scientific method gathers data from observations. This data could be analysed and organized into a hypothesis. This hypothesis might conflict with a previous widely-held hypothesis. If such a new hypothesis should be widely accepted it could create a new Law which might displace an earlier Law. This new Law would stand until the discovery of other data that disqualifies it, giving rise to new hypotheses and a new Law. All scientific progress follows this trajectory of doubting received wisdom and revising the Laws of Science. Thus Newton's Law of Gravitation was modified by Einstein's Theories of Relativity which in turn were modified by Quantum Theory where a world of probability has replaced certainty. Initially Einstein rejected quantum theory, saying "God does not roll dice!", but later, to his credit, he came to admit the elegance and empowerment that springs from the uncertainty embraced by quantum theory.

What I learned in school as "The Laws of Science" are all changed. However these changes have opened up new and exciting possibilities undreamed-of at the time—the transistor, the laser, nuclear power, and the gravitational lens which bends light to reveal deep-space objects. All scientific research is based on doubt. It shakes at the foundations of established laws, hoping to establish new laws or create new products. Doubting opens up new possibilities. Without doubting there would be no scientific progress.

Most scientists doubt the existence of God, or to put it more precisely, they hold that in quantum terms the probability that God exists is very small. Of course if God should choose to reveal His existence to Man (as opposed to Man undertaking this task for Him) scientists would consider this to be new data and revise their opinion as to His non-existence; but that has not happened yet.

What about that small percentage of scientists who also profess a religious belief? Some manage to compartmentalize their lives, being rational in the laboratory and religious in church. I too can manage this transition: I become a devout Roman Catholic for the 110 minute duration of a performance of Bach's Mass in B Minor (or for 130 minutes if there was an intermission) and when teaching a class I can take on the liberal catholic (note the small "c"!) mindset that best serves the students of the institution where I am employed. Some scientists are unable to make such a transition and seek a

Great Universal Theory which probably cannot exist, because religion and science are so opposite, the one demanding belief and the other demanding doubt.

There have been attempts to patch over this divide, to give religion a gloss of rationality. I don't think any of them has been successful. In 2003 a book "Modern Physics and Ancient Faith" was published by Notre Dame Press. The author, Stephen M. Barr is a professor of physics and astronomy at the University of Delaware, and a Roman Catholic. The title of the book sounds promising, but in that it is deceptive: it implies that the book discovers some sort of equivalence or mutual support between physics and faith, but on opening the book we find that this is not the case. The book is much more an attack on materialism. Its logic is tortuous and its arguments fallacious, but I will attempt to unpack them . . .

1. Faith and materialism are opposites — fair enough.

2. Recent developments in science show a departure from materialism: Newton's view of a universe of billiard balls has been supplanted by Gödel, Eisenberg, and Planck into an indeterminate realm of probabilities — OK.

3. Thus faith and science are compatible.

That is a false syllogism as it asserts an affirmative conclusion from a negative premise: If either premise (1 or 2) is negative, the conclusion (3) must also be negative. To illustrate the symbolic illogic of this argument it can be expressed as:

Faith ≠ Materialism, Science ≠ Materialism, therefore Faith = Science.

A similar argument is lodged in the aphorism "My enemy's enemy is my friend." Recent events in the Arab world have proved this to be profoundly untrue — we have found that people that hate one another are perfectly capable of hating us too. The title of Barr's book implies a harmonious relationship between physics and faith, between science and religion, but the content fails to deliver. In fact 80% of the book is an attack on materialism which is irrelevant. None of the scientists I know, and none of the atheists I know, is a materialist—all are moved by the grace and wonder of our world. The other 20% of the book is a peppering of scientific articles and diagrams to give the book an impressive academic persona. It impressed the Holy Father. In 2007 Pope Benedict XVI awarded the author a Benerementi Medal, the highest honor awarded to laymen "for services to the Catholic Church." This was a strange award because those held in highest regard by the Catholic Church, the Saints, achieved that status by being responsible for miracles which somehow thwarted the laws of science.

Science is founded on doubt, but people of faith do not have these doubts. They live in a world where they bask in the comfort of certainty. For those professing a Christian faith "Faith is the substance of things hoped-for, the evidence of things not seen"[1]; or in the words of Mark Twain's schoolboy[2] "Faith is believing what you know ain't so!"

When I admitted this landscape of doubt to John Clarke, a colleague at Trinity College who shares an office with me and who shares his initials with an even greater Teacher, John said "It's smart to be a person of faith. If your belief in Eternal Life turns out to be true you benefit from it, and if it's not true you have not lost anything." In this he echoed the reasoning behind Pascal's Wager.

Blaise Pascal (1623–1662), a French scientist and mathematician, expressed the same sentiments in his Pensées[3] as a four-cell matrix. The two columns represent the possibilities that God exists or God does not exist. The two rows represent belief and unbelief. Pascal demanded that you wager either that God exists or God does not exist—holding that a refusal to wager is itself a bet that God does not exist.

The table illustrates that if you believe in God, and God exists, you gain eternal life; while if you believe in a God that does not exist you have not lost or gained anything.

PASCAL'S WAGER		
	God Exists	God does not Exist
Belief in God	Infinite Gain (Heaven)	No Loss
Non-Belief	Infinite Loss (Hell)	No Gain

Fig. 1. A matrix tabulation of the options offered by Pascal's Wager.

However if you choose not to believe in God, and God exists, you risk losing everything through eternal damnation, but if God does not exist you have not lost or gained anything. From this Pascal deduced that, even though we can never know for sure whether God exists or not, the wise course to follow is to be a believer.

The Pascal Conspiracy
Pascal was a brilliant scientist but as a punter he had his limitations. He did not consider that there could be more than one horse in the race. Pascal is staking everything on the Pope's entry to win, but the field is huge: Allah, Jehovah, Krishna, Buddha, Baal, Ra, to name just a few of the favourites. Even after studying form (a.k.a. Comparative Religion) and eliminating all the unlikely contenders there are

still more options than are offered in the Kentucky Derby. How to choose? ... it's a horse race.

If there's just one horse in the race the result is predictable, but with so many entrants it's anybody's guess. If Pascal guessed wrong he could arrive at the Pearly Gates only to receive a rough reception from Thor, Zeus, the Gitchi Manitou or whoever else is in charge. And then, even if he had backed the right God, a win would not necessarily lead to a pay-off.

An additional incongruity is that Pascal was a Jansenist, that is, he was a follower of the teachings of St. Augustine of Hippo as professed by Cornelius Jansen (1585-1638). The teachings of St. Augustine included the doctrine of original sin, which is logical if one accepts as real a reported conversation between two nudists and a talking snake (you're guilty before you start) and pre-destination (God has already decided your destination and there's nothing you can do about it). So backing the winner could still result in infinite loss. Pascal was prepared for this, saying "I would prefer an intelligent hell to a stupid paradise."

These doctrines ran counter to the current teachings of the Catholic Church, which held that the grace of salvation is available to all subscribers, like universal health care. It would limit their customer base and be bad for their bottom line to admit otherwise. Without the promise of a pay-off why would anyone put up with all the aggravation? There was not much the Church could do about St. Augustine who had already been beatified, but Cornelius Jansen was still vulnerable. The Jesuits led the intellectual attack, accusing the Jansenists of being heretical Calvinists. There was some substance to this as Calvin too had accepted some of St. Augustine's views, but the Jansenists were not about launching a second Reformation; they just sought more clarity in doctrine. Many French intellectuals rallied to the cause, and Pascal engaged with the Jesuits in a series of sardonic papers mocking their position. The battle lasted for years, until the Pope was persuaded to put an end to it. On May 31, 1653 Pope Innocent X issued the bull *Cum Occasione,* and Jansenism's supporters suffered a decisive defeat.

Even though the Jansenists, or most of them, returned to the bosom of the Holy Catholic Church it was hard for them to accept that an all-powerful God could be coerced by humans into accepting into Heaven all applicants who had been issued with satisfactory immigration papers. Pascal was still aware of the possibility that even if one wagered correctly on the existence of the God of the Catholic Church there was no evidence that that Deity was obliged to accept all comers, further reducing the odds of winning. In Pascal's matrix the probability of a believer achieving the "infinite gain" of eternal life is not 100%. It is tempered by the product of the improbability of betting on the existence of the right God, multiplied by the improbability of that God complying with every human request for admission. Pascal was a skilled mathematician, he must have realized these limitations. Why would he present an argument so full of holes?

Here's the thing. As a scientist Pascal had an intimate acquaintance with holes. He rejected the conventional wisdom that every hole had to be filled with something—that a vacuum could not exist. At that time the Platonic adage "Nature abhors a vacuum" had been raised to the status of being a Law of Science. This "Law" did have its usefulness in explaining why when you suck on a drinking straw and risk creating—Oh horrors!—a vacuum, Nature rushes to your aid and defies gravity by giving you a mouthful of lemonade. Pascal offered the more elegant theory that due to gravitation the atmosphere exerts pressure, and it is the pressure of the atmosphere on the surface of the liquid in the glass that forces it up the straw and into the mouth.

To demonstrate the pressure of the atmosphere, in 1648 Pascal performed an experiment in Paris. He took several one-metre glass tubes sealed at one end and filled them with mercury. He up-ended the tubes and immersed the open ends in a dish of mercury. The mercury no longer filled the tubes to the top; it had partly slid down leaving empty spaces at the top. He marked the point to which levels of the surfaces of the mercury in the tubes had fallen, about 76 centimeters, creating a vacuum above its surface. He then took this apparatus to the top of the bell tower at the church of Saint-Jacques-de-la-Boucherie, a height of about fifty meters, and noted that the level of the mercury had dropped from the value it had had at street level. From this he deduced both the pressure of the atmosphere and the presence of the vacuum and today atmospheric pressure is measured in kilopascals in his honor.

Up to that point it had been postulated that Outer Space was filled with an imaginary substance called the ether, or æther, to give it its more classy spelling. This conjecture derived from the human proclivity to devise something to fill up all empty spaces with something. However there was no way in which anyone could see how some of this æther could have gotten into Pascal's sealed glass tube, so it was conceded that he had indeed created a vacuum that was truly empty.

The same reasoning that had created a non-existent æther to fill a vacuum also created a God to fill up the empty spaces beyond Space, and the empty times before and after Time. In doubting the existence of the one was Pascal also doubting the other? Like most modern scientists was Pascal also an atheist? This was not something that could be proclaimed in Seventeenth Century France where the Inquisition was still an agency for ensuring conformity. The only way the conspirators could offer alternatives to the dogma of the Catholic Church was to publish papers ostensibly supporting the dogma, but by using arguments so full of holes as to invite a more-critical examination.

If this was Pascal's purpose, to filter out of dogma some of the less-supportable items of doctrine, he achieved only moderate success. He over-estimated the intelligence of his readers, not realising how far his intelligence outstripped theirs, and for some people his underhand assault on credulity was accepted at face value and became an affirmation of the faith. In this instance, to quote Paul Claudel[4], "Even the worst can not be relied on".

Celestial Life Insurance

Pascal's Wager offered a winner a future of bliss. This ensuring against importunate perils is the purview of the insurance industry. So-called life insurance, which is really death insurance, undertakes to pay a large sum of money to the policy holder on the death of the insured. Thus it is in the interest of the insurer for the insured to live as long as possible in order to collect the maximum number of premiums, and after a long life inflation will have reduced the initial value of the eventual payout to a much smaller sum. No wonder insurance companies are so rich. Essentially, insurance companies are betting that you will live to a ripe old age. Conversely, the insured is betting that he will die in the short term. Every year that the insured person survives he will say "Dammit! I'm still alive! I've lost again! Now I will have to pay another year's premium!" Pascal's Wager offers the possibility of eternal life, a prospect that would cause life insurance companies to salivate, but what would the premiums be? In my case, even if I wanted eternal life (which I don't) I would consider them to be too expensive. In order to be a candidate for eternal life I would have to give up intelligence, logic, autonomy, courage. I would have to be subservient to trumped-up authority and accept all sorts of irrationality as gospel. I would have to assent to arguments that are essentially untenable. I would have to abandon all intelligence. I would have to assert a spurious certainty in a context of ignorance. This price would be much too high, for what does it profit a man to forfeit his whole world and gain an immortality he does not particularly want? Thanks, but no thanks.

NOTES for Chapter One

[1] Epistle to the Romans 11:1
[2] Mark Twain *Following the Equator*, Pudd'nhead Wilson's Calendar, 1897.
[3] Blaise Pascal *Pensees* trans: *W. F. Trotter*, Introduction by T. S. Eliot. J.M. Dent, 1931.
[4] Paul Claudel, prologue to *Le Soulier de Satin*, 1929.

CHAPTER TWO

Do Atheists have Souls?

When I was about five years old my maternal grandmother told me that she had been taught that "your soul is your breath". I accepted her statement; that the soul is composed of moist air, perfumed sometimes with breath mints or cough drops.

Years later I learned that in both Hinduism and Buddhism breath is considered to be an actual body within the body. It is equated to a life energy force, to Prajna or the Chinese Chi. This gave the concept a cultural context, but did little more to define it.

Then, while assembling the words for this book, I had a realisation in which I fused these two concepts. Breath is composed of air, a mixture of 21% oxygen, 78% nitrogen with other gases comprising the other 1%, but air becomes breath only when it is in the body. Air inhaled becomes breath; breath exhaled becomes air. Breath is the individuation of a small portion of the atmosphere that surrounds the planet. Breath, to exist, needs a living body. It is a token of life. The cry of a newborn is the sign that a new life has begun. The cessation of breathing is a sign that life has departed. I have no concept of having had any individual existence (or soul, if you like) before I was born—I think most people share that insight. Like breath, the soul requires a living body, what the Buddhists call a sentient being. When breath is exhaled it ceases to exist as breath. It becomes reunited with the atmosphere from which it came. From this I deduced that just as the individual soul had no existence before birth I see no reason why it should continue to have an existence after death. If the soul is a form of individuation of a universal consciousness which has migrated into a living body I see no reason why it should not return to its source when the body stops living, just as breath returns to the atmosphere — recycling rather than land-fill. A dead body often appears to be even more dead than something that never lived — a rock or a rocking-chair. These exist as celebrations of the forces that created them, while a dead body is just an initial stage of compost.

Death forces on us a realization that our lives are finite, and for many of us it arrives before we are ready for it. This makes an afterlife an attractive prospect for many — a second kick at the can, a second chance to right wrongs or achieve something, a compensation for a lifetime of suffering, an opportunity for fulfillment, a reunion where broken relationships can be restored, a resolution of disappointments. However, this has a downside: if we are going to have an opportunity to fix things up in the sweet bye-and-bye we don't need to be so concerned about messing things up during our temporary presence in the here-and-now. For the Atheist the here-and-now takes on a much greater importance: that of being all-there-is. There's just one kick at the can, just one opportunity to get things right, so for the Atheist the future is now, which makes life more exciting. I am writing these words as fast as I can, a rush to reach "The End" before I reach my end, because I have already passed my "best before" date, and I want to be able to complete these pages so I can share them with you. If you are reading this it means I got in under the wire. In a short story[5] Tennessee Williams wrote "Death has never been much in the way of completion." This accounts for a lot of the sadness around death. Death is an end, an end that often finishes life before we are finished with living. Death has no impact on what we have completed; it just frustrates what we still need to do: the letter not written, the love not embraced, the garden not tended, the dog not fed, the meal prepared but not cooked, the wine poured but not drunk—that is where the sadness lies.

In my grandmother's house there were two texts on either side of the fireplace. One read "I am the Bread of Life"[6], but it was done with such fancy gothick lettering I thought the initial "I" was a "J". It still made sense, perhaps more sense, as an invocation to spread strawberry jam on whatever crusts life has to offer us, to live life to the full. The other text was titled "I Shall Not Pass This Way Again"[7]. It was a poem that echoed those sentiments . . .

> "I shall pass this way but once;
> Any good that I can do or any kindness I can
>   show to any human being; let me do it now.
> Let me not defer nor neglect it,
> For I shall not pass this way again."

This poem is an inspiration, an invitation to live one's life in the immediate present, as if there were no prospect for revisions in a later eternal life. It is a commitment to care for the environment we have inherited and to render ourselves more extensively serviceable to our fellow creatures. One does not have to have a God in order to strive to achieve this. One does not have to have a God in order to have a soul. We have a job in the here-and-now, and with the end of life that job will be ended, even if it is not completed.

The theological concept that I find to be the most elegant, the most rational, and with the fewest sentimental accretions, is that the soul, like the breath, is the personal individuation of a universal consciousness. The soul partners the life in the body, and at the end of that life it returns to whence it came. This is a completely natural process; it does not require the intervention of a God. It does not project an everlasting life into an eternity that must be getting overcrowded. The aspect of eternal life which it does permit is as eternal as the persistence of memory in other humans. Thus I cannot deny that Shakespeare is still offering new insights into relationships in our present society, and Glen Gould continues to reveal hidden concordances in the Goldberg Variations. For many (but not for me) Elvis lives. To quote W.H. Auden[8]

> "Time that is intolerant
>   of the brave and innocent,
> And indifferent in a week
>   to a beautiful physique
> Worships language and forgives
>   everyone by whom it lives."

When I visit one of the Wren churches in London I am immediately in a connection with Sir Christopher, and with all those who have worshiped there in the past. We co-exist in a pool of consciousness. How else to explain the impact of a work of art? . . . except to say that a spiritual expression of the universal soul that infuses the living body may also become embedded in physical reality. Such a construct could be the channel for empathy, intuition, inspiration, synchronicity, and perhaps love.

A Universal Consciousness

The concept of an infinite intelligence, a universal consciousness that permeates all human beings, lies at the heart of the New Thought movement, a spiritual movement which developed in the United States in the 19th century. It was based on the teachings of Phineas Parkhurst Quimby (1802–1866). Quimby lived in Belfast, Maine, where he plied his trade as a clockmaker, but he developed a much wider reputation as a healer. Many of those who came to him for consultations had chronic conditions, or had been pronounced incurable by the medical profession. His process was to teach that we are spiritual beings connected by our thoughts to a vast and infinite world of the spirit. We are part of a whole, and the part must be identical with the whole. Whatever we create in the part, the whole will also manifest. Thus if we are preoccupied with sickness or insufficiency our thoughts will attract those qualities into our lives, so to achieve healing we should train our thinking to hold only thoughts of health, prosperity and joy. Because our conscious minds are individual expressions of a universal mind that is omnipotent, omniscient and omnipresent, holding these thoughts of health, prosperity and joy in our individual minds will cause their qualities to materialize in our individual lives.

This concept is supported by the thought of René Descarte's 1637 aphorism "Cogito, ergo sum" or "I think, therefore I am". This is not just a recital of two parallel activities: thinking and being. The word "therefore" implies that my thoughts are a necessary condition for my being. And what are my thoughts? They are the thoughts I have selected to entertain out of all the possible thoughts in the universe. I don't take thoughts from a Universal Mind, I merely reproduce them. My thinking of a thought does not deprive somebody else. The protocol is "Copy and Paste", not "Cut and Paste". My thoughts, and therefore my existence, are an individuation, a sampling, of all available thought. Thoughts are created and held in the mind. My mind is a function of my brain, which for its operation requires a constant supply of oxygenated blood. Thus when my heart stops delivering that nutrient my mind will cease to function, I will no longer have thoughts, and the life of "I" will end. But by taking thoughts for my own I have not reduced the thoughts of a Universal Mind; it's a situation similar to accessing an e-book which is still available to other readers, as opposed to borrowing a library book which depletes the stacks. Thus it is a convenience to think that at the end of my life all thought will return to the source from which it came. This concept was supported by Sam Harris[9], a neuroscientist who has investigated mental function. Harris entertained the possibility that consciousness could exist outside of [and beyond] the human brain. This allows for the possibility that such disconnected consciousness could be available to other humans, lending support to Haanel's concept of a Universal Mind.

This is the theme of the New Thought movement: by accepting a new thought I create a new me. By selecting those new thoughts that are supportive and rejecting those that are negative I can create a new me the way I want me to be. This transformation is at the heart of all religions. Most of them provide a god who has the authority to tell you what those new thoughts should be, but the process works perfectly well, perhaps better, if no god is involved. Atheists can create their lives the way they want them to be, without the baggage of belief. Some have chosen to regard Quimby's concept of a universal consciousness as a declaration of the presence of God; others regard it as referring to a pool of infinite intelligence, the source of all wisdom. The New Thought movement has found many expressions, ranging from religious gatherings where the Infinite is identified with God to discussion groups which pursue a more philosophical path. These expressions are not in conflict, they are differing interpretations of the same concept. God is presented in them almost as a metaphor—as a personalisation of an abstract principle.

The God, as presented by some of the more benign TV Evangelists such as Robert H. Schuller and Joel Osteen, has taken on the role of a Personal Trainer, cheering us on as we strive for perfection. They preach to thousands (Joel Osteen fills Yankee Stadium) but television can expand their thrust to

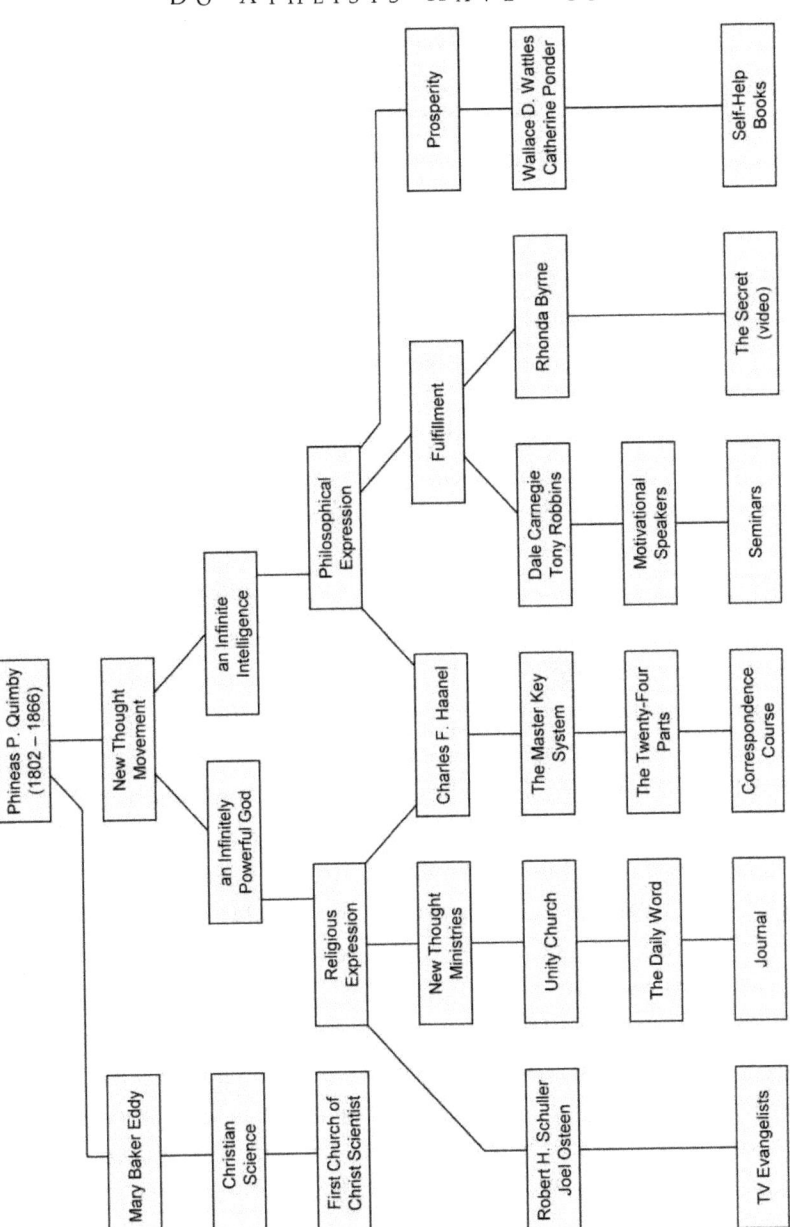

Fig. 2. Expressions of the New Thought Movement

millions, delivering a message of hope and encouragement. In their broadcasts there are occasional references to texts taken from scripture but these are illustrations, not dogma, so there is nothing in them to offend the atheist if one is prepared to separate the rhetoric from the message. Their approach is distinct from that of some other Evangelists who take a more hard-line approach, offering as the goal not fulfillment in this life but salvation in a future one.

At the opposite pole the Unity Church delivers the same message to individuals. Silent Unity[10] is a prayer ministry that publishes The Daily Word, a bi-monthly journal of focus and meditation, offering hope, affirmation and inspiration to over two million individuals. Its message is a more pro-active version of the horoscopes which appear daily in many newspapers; listing not how our lives are influenced by the stars but how we may influence our lives by focusing on an aspect of the good. For every day of the week The Daily Word offers a key word, a picture with romantic overtones, a sentence taken from scripture, a brief homily and a non-denominational prayer. This serves to set each day in a spiritual context, and many get great comfort from this. The Daily Word has been translated into several languages and has been published continuously since 1924.

There are other expressions of the New Thought movement which do not identify the Source with God, or choose to mention Him only very sparingly. Their focus is on the philosophical construct of an all-pervading energy into which an individual can tap by consciously directed thought, opening a door to fulfillment and/or prosperity. Some exponents such as Wallace D. Wattles (The Science of Getting Rich) and Catherine Ponder (The Dynamic Laws of Prosperity) focus on attracting wealth by adopting an attitude of sufficiency. Others such as Dale Carnegie and Tony Robbins are exponents of the growth movement, applying the teaching to a wider field, offering lectures, seminars and workshops to promote accomplishment, satisfaction and success. Some of these leaders have acquired large followings, as did the prophets of old, leading seminars such as Est, or The Legacy Weekend.

The most elegant expression of the enlightenment offered by the New Thought movement is The Master Key System devised by Charles F. Haanel (1866 – 1949) a St. Louis, MO business man. Haanel holds that thought is constructive, and human thought is the spiritual power of the cosmos operating through its creature, Man. In "The Master Key" he instructs the reader in how to acknowledge the existence of that power and use it both constructively and creatively. The things and conditions we desire to become realities we must first create in thought. This is the course that is also recommended in Philippians 4:8 :

> "Finally, brethren, whatsoever things are true, whatsoever things are honest, whatsoever things are just, whatsoever things are pure, whatsoever things are lovely, whatsoever things are of good report; if there be any virtue, and if there be any praise, think on these things."

The Master Key System may be seen as an expression which combines both the religious and the philosophical outpourings of the New Thought movement. Haanel illustrates the ecumenism of his thesis by offering alternate interpretations[11]. He writes . . .

> "The following statement is of great importance, so I will put it in several ways, so that you cannot fail to get the full significance of it.
> "If you are religiously inclined, I would say, you can let your light shine.

"If your mind has a bias toward physical science, I would say you can energize the central nervous system; or . . .

"If you prefer the strictly scientific interpretation, I will say that you can impress your subconscious mind."

"All truth is the same, whether stated in modern scientific terms or in the language of apostolic times. There are timid souls who fail to realize that the very completeness of truth requires various statements — that no one human formula will show every side of it."

Haanel presented the Master Key System in the form of a twenty-four part correspondence course: The Twenty-Four Parts. For ten dollars (equivalent to several hundred dollars at present values) a subscriber would receive a package in the mail each week for twenty four weeks. It was immensely popular, and is said to have inspired many of the entrepreneurs of Silicon Valley. This information is now available on-line, but there were advantages to the original format in that it slowed down assimilation, allowing time for each lesson to be absorbed and practised before the next one arrived. Perhaps we need that format even more in today's speeded-up lifestyle, where attention spans are limited and inter-personal communication is tweeted in the form of 140-character sound bites. Rhonda Byrne has responded to the demands of today's life-style by creating a 90-minute video with the title "The Secret". It includes excursions into mythology (The Emerald Tablets of Thoth), conspiracy theories (What the bosses don't want you to know), and comments by fifty-five motivational guru's, all presented with the surging soundscape and graphic effects of a video game. It's had great popular success, but its ease of access has reduced its effectiveness. Those who wish to meditate on its message, to study it in depth, have to view the whole ninety minutes over again, to be once more swept along its frantic trajectory. Some people, in order to attain the teaching, have watched the video over fifty times. For others, a single exposure to the video offered an adequate injection of enlightenment that would last for a couple of weeks, then off on another quest for perfection.

"The Secret" is also being published as a book[12], the book of the movie. It shares with the video the same ornate graphic style. An attempt is made to give the book an historic look—the pages are all browned at the edges and the text is printed over palimpsest erasures, ghost images of earlier entries; it almost smells of ancient documents gathering dust in musty old libraries: instant ancestry. Atheists, being purists, might find this off-putting, analogous to the attempt by religious organisations to give their preachers a provenance by dressing them up in robes that might have been fashionable five centuries ago. The book itself has the same fractured trajectory as the video; hundreds of tweets by an assembly of luminaries which can be read in almost any order. The ease of access contributes to the book's commercial success but mitigates its effectiveness as a force for change in the world. That which floats so easily into the mind can just as easily float out. Disciplining the mind to reshape its reality requires hard work.

Charles Haanel, in The Twenty-Four Parts, offers instruction in how to master the mind, how we should work to control our thoughts. A discipline that should be within our grasp but might be surprisingly difficult would be to schedule reading the on-line version of The Twenty-Four Parts as if it were a weekly mail-drop; opening up a new section no more frequently than once a week. I've tried to do that—it's not that easy. All the flowerings of the New Thought movement, the various pathways to fulfillment, have been of service to atheists. Their authors seek to appeal to all humanity, not just those who have adopted a particular belief system, so they take care that when they make any religious references these are just to illustrate a point, like the pictures in story books; and looking back on my own childhood I never appreciated a book with a lot of pictures—the images offered to the imagination by the text were way richer than anything provided by the illustrator. The evangelists who are expounding the principles of the New Thought movement (although few would admit it) offer a generic enlightenment. This is necessary if they wish their appeal to extend beyond the sectarian interests of a particular denomination. The God that they invoke is generic, a No-Name brand that has limited advertised presence. The prayer that ends one of Joel Osteen's 30-minute broadcasts takes up less than ten seconds of air time . . . "Will you pray with me? Lord Jesus, I repent of my sins, Come into my heart. I make you my Lord and Savior. Amen". Without being cynical I would note that more time is devoted to fundraising and organisational notices than is given to direct prayer to a deity. This an atheist can forgive, while deriving benefit from the rest of the presentation.

Atheists are spiritual beings. This might be difficult for some people of faith to accept if they regard their own spirituality as an essential adhesion to a structure of codified beliefs and without such advantages man is merely an assemblage of animated meat. It is plain to me that man is a spiritual being, and those who identify with a rigid system of beliefs through which they regard the world are perhaps less aware of this. If we choose to regard the spiritual world through a filter of a rigid system of beliefs we impose our own materialist limits on the universal thrust of the spirit. This danger was pointed out by Chögyam Trungpa[13], a Tibetan Buddhist teacher in his 1973 book "Cutting Through Spiritual Materialism". He wrote:

"Are the great spiritual teachings really advocating that we fight evil because we are on the side of light, the side of peace? Are they telling us to fight against that other 'undesirable' side, the bad and the black. That is a big question. If there is wisdom in the sacred teachings, there should not be any war.."

New Thought would assert that man is primarily a spiritual being, or rather that man is the individual expression of a universal spirit in a human body. Great strength is enabled by nurturing that connection. One of the most severe forms of institutional punishment is solitary confinement, where there is no communication with other humans. Those who are most able to withstand such mistreatment are the ones who are most in touch with their spiritual nature and its connection to a world of spirit that is not confined by prison walls.

Mary Baker Eddy, the founder of Christian Science, was one of Quimby's students when she was a very sick person. Under his guidance she was healed, but the severity of her affliction left her with a distorted view of Quimby's principles. Instead of embracing health she became preoccupied with combating "the illusion of disease", an illusion that must be defeated by prayer. That became the focus of the Church of Christ Scientist. The church rejects medical interventions altogether. Quimby's concept of an infinite universal intelligence she interpreted as "God", and to give God a Christian vector she held that by rejecting drugs, medicines, and hygiene she was following Christ's example, as Jesus did not use those modalities when He was healing people. Thus Christian Science became a church with all the trimmings: buildings, preachers, congregations, worship services, prayer books, doctrine and exemption from taxation. The faith's guiding textbook[14] forbids mixing medical care with the healing rituals of Christian Science, arguing that sickness is an illusion that can be corrected by prayer alone. It did not always work, and deaths have resulted from parents refusing to let their children have the medical interventions that could have saved them.

Christian Science can not be regarded as an outcome of the New Thought movement. Its doctrine is a very narrow reading of Christ's ministry, and its practice is a flawed application of New Thought principles. The failures of Christian Science illustrate Carl Gustav Jung's aphorism "What we resist persists". We see similar failures in the conduct of various wars: The War on Drugs provides no alternative to stupefaction. The battle cry "Fight Cancer" ensures that cancer will remain a formidable foe. Vast sums have been expended in the War on Poverty. Despite its good intentions "The Hunger Project™" will never end starvation. The War on Terror has not made us less afraid. New thinking is needed, but even New Thought will not be useful if it's role is seen as to counter other established philosophies. Why is it so hard to love the good?

NOTES for Chapter Two

[5] Tennessee Williams, One Arm and Other Stories, 1967 New Directions
[6] John 6:35
[7] Translation of Etienne de Grellet (1773-1855); Quaker Missionary
[8] In memory of W. B. Yeats, The Collected Poetry of W. H. Auden, 1945, Random House.
[9] Sam Harris, Waking Up, a Guide to Spirituality without Religion. 2014, Simon and Schuster
[10] Silent Unity, 1901 NW Blue Parkway, Unity Village, MO, USA.
[11] Charles F. Haanel, The Twenty Four Parts, 1912
[12] Rhonda Byrne, The Secret. 2006, Simon & Schuster.
[13] Chogyam Trungpa, Cutting Through Spiritual Materialism, 1973 Shambhala Publications
[14] Science and Health, with a Key to the Scriptures (1875)

CHAPTER THREE
Faith or Reason?

This was the subject of a great medieval debate between Anselm (an Archbishop of Canterbury from 1093 to 1109, who later became Saint Anselm) and Peter Abelard (formerly his pupil, and most noted for his life-long romance with Heloïse). Anselm (1033-1109) in his Proslogion[15], staked out his position as "I believe in order that I may understand", a maxim that he inherited from St. Augustine of Hippo[16]. He chose to experience the world through the prism of his faith, a prism that overlays a rainbow of colors on an image, but at the risk of some distortion. This mindset ensures that what Anselm considers to be the objective world will be totally consistent with his beliefs—a closed system. Any inconsistency will have a theological explanation.

Abelard (1079–1142), considered one of the greatest thinkers of the twelfth century, took the opposite tack, saying "I understand, so that I may believe". He upheld the principle that the truths of faith and reason must be in agreement, but when there is any conflict he demanded that reason must have precedence. It is faith that has to adapt, i.e. the church must re-evaluate the meaning of its teachings when they fail to measure up to reason. Abelard founded a school in Paris to expound these principles, but his questioning matters of faith angered some of the members of the church establishment. His teachings were controversial, and he was repeatedly charged with heresy. If I am perceived as having a similar role in these pages I could face a similar fate. However when

Abelard not only questioned the doctrine of the Holy Trinity but offered his own version of it he had gone too far. He proposed that the Holy Trinity was not a triune god comprising Father, Son, and Holy Ghost but could be regarded as a representation of God's power, wisdom, and love. For this he was silenced by Pope Innocent II who issued

Fig. 3. Diocesan Disagreements

an order condemning him to perpetual silence and confinement to a monastery. That was the usual penalty for heresy at that time. On his way to Rome to defend himself he died at age sixty-three. However none of these measures of suppression succeeded. Abelard's ideas are now more widespread than ever, and despite his castration by an uncle of Heloïse his love affair with her continued throughout his lifetime, and now in Paris they lie together in the Père Lachaise Cemetery.

Abelard found difficulty in resolving the discrepancies between the beliefs that were required of him and his more rational insights; a conflict also experienced by Alice[17] during her sojourn in Wonderland, when she remarked (to the White Queen):

> "There's no use trying; one can't believe impossible things."
>
> "I daresay you haven't had much practice," said the Queen. "When I was younger, I always did it for half an hour a day. Why, sometimes I've believed as many as six impossible things before breakfast."

We all choose our beliefs, but we are not totally free in that regard. We are influenced by our families, communities, nations, by the cultures and traditions they support. Nobody will tell you what to order in an Indian restaurant, you have freedom of choice, but satisfaction will be limited if you order chop suey. For that you have put on your coat, leave the restaurant, and go across the street.

The world offers many choices of religion. Maps of the world may be colored-in to indicate the predominant locations of all the major religions, but another map would be required to indicate (in shades of grey, grading to black) all major locations of atheism. A separate map would be required because those areas overlay one another, it's not a zero-sum—some people who are atheists are religious, even if they do not have faith. Colors on the map indicate that theology could be a geographic phenomenon, making it difficult for people of faith to assert that their own faith choice represents the unique and only truth; surely a bit of doubt must creep in somewhere? But that does not stop them, the more tenuous the argument the more strenuously it is supported. Perhaps the logic that supports faith is so fragile it needs the rigidity of unthinking conformity.

People of faith assert that their faith is the one true faith, their path the right path, their color on the map the correct color for all maps. The map shows many different colors, at least 4,200 of them[18], it's rainbow-hued like the color chart issued by a paint manufacturer, and since all are agreed there can be only one right answer it follows that in that grouping at least 4,199 must be wrong, a vast sea of error. Most people of faith must be mistaken. It could be argued that all these deities are different forms of the same God, but I don't see anybody buying that argument. That argument only applies to other people's Gods, which are seen as inferior versions of our own God. Over the centuries oceans of blood have been shed to decide which of these different versions is the right one.

Believing, in spite of not seeing, is the path of faith. This is supported in John Mason Neale's translation of the 15th Century hymn "O Filii et Filiæ" (I give the Latin text with the same rhyme scheme in a footnote[19]; this is a scholarly work:)

"How blessed are they who have not seen,
And yet whose faith has constant been;
For they eternal life shall win.
Alleluia!"

In this context the sheer lack of evidence is seen as a virtue, a blessing. It would be no great achievement to believe something that is obviously true. In this context it is a virtue to believe something where there is minimal supporting evidence, and the less evidence there is the greater the virtue. The greatest virtue of all is accorded to faith where there is no supporting evidence at all. Because faith is not evidence-based it can have an eternal presence. It will not be shifted by any new evidence that might appear, or by whatever might occur in the future. The text is based on a quotation of Jesus in John 20:29.

> "Because you have seen me, you have believed; blessed are those who have not seen and yet have believed."

This is a recursive text, proceeding by a circular argument. These words of encouragement were reported as having been spoken by Jesus after He had died; so one has to have faith in order to gain that faith. Here is the narrative in which the passage occurs . . .

Eleven days after the death of Jesus the disciples are meeting in a locked room. We are told repeatedly that the doors are locked, and Jesus floats in (through walls or doors) and invites Thomas (who had been doubting the possibility of a post-mortem messiah) to poke at His wounds to verify His reality, after which He delivers the above phrase. There are some problems with this scenario. First, the text was written fifty years after the event, and there are no corroborations for the events it records. Wiki would say "citation needed". Second, Jesus is presented as an insubstantial wraith that can float through walls but then be solid enough to be poked and prodded by Thomas.

Next, it is a scholarly text that does not sound like Jesus voice at all. Jesus' speech was rich in aphorisms, parables and humor, as noted by the forty scholars of the Jesus Seminar[20]. The speeches attributed to Jesus in John's Gospel read like homilies preached to some congregation over the horizon. In some bibles, such as the NIV Study Bible[21], and especially in the inerrant ones, the words of Jesus are printed in red. In "The Five Gospels" the words of Jesus are also color coded — red is preserved for those words most likely spoken by Jesus in a form close to the one appearing. Where there was less certainty pink was employed (as a weaker form of red).

Words that scholars assumed not to have originated with Jesus, but were the construction of some scribe, appear in grey or black—grey if the sentiments could have been made by Jesus and black if that was unlikely. All the words attributed to Jesus in John's Gospel are in the black category, indicating the probability that they are a literary construct rather than a record of a conversation with an historical Jesus. They have the measured tones one can hear in a million sermons.

It is by no means certain, then, from the wording in that passage, that Jesus has maintained that believing alone will secure salvation, that could be the opinion of a scribe (or an editor!) and it would be a terrible thing to find out, too late, that good works were also a requirement. This is illustrated in a parable[22] where a father ordered two of his sons to work in the vineyard. One said "I will do it" and did not, the other said "I will not do it" and yet he did. Which son obeyed his father? Obviously the second one, the one who valued works over proclamations.

Belief is the acceptance of a statement as being true. Belief is a choice; but there are two categories of truth from which one may choose: two ways in which a statement may be claimed to be true. To distinguish these categories I will call them permanent truths and provisional truths. Permanent truths are created by making a declaration, and provisional truths are deduced from experience. Permanent truths are unchanging. They were created without recourse to experiment, experience or logic so those tools cannot be used to modify them. Provisional truths are changing all the time as the frontiers of knowledge and experience advance. Religious or artistic statements are permanent truths; scientific or logical statements are provisional truths. Perhaps it is an error to call scientific statements truths of any sort. Martin Johnson[23] writes "Science is the study where we neither know nor care whether what we say is true." Provisional truths are "what-works-for-now", statements that can be organized into a coherent system, but over time that system itself could change.

Permanent truths may be created by popes, politicians, prophets, promoters, pundits, or those transcribing the Word of God, if not God Himself. The higher the regard for the status of the authority doing the declaring the more power is vested in that truth. These truths are permanent because they cannot be altered. Sometimes they are called eternal truths, as if this gives them additional authority. They could need it, because so many people have been declaring so many things there are many permanent truths in competition with one another. They don't agree with one another, they vary in content, but each one is constant through time. It is this feature of being unchanging that gives them their permanent quality. They cannot be changed but any one of them could be overlain by another even-more-true permanent truth. We, all of us, change our selections of permanent truths as we mature. Some of us upgrade our infantile beliefs, and some of us discard them.

People of faith have chosen permanent truths which they choose to govern their lives. Atheists choose to believe in a single cluster of provisional truths, a cluster which may be adjusted over time. There are many permanent truths to choose from, so the truth that is selected by a person of faith is a subjective choice. Permanent truth is absolute, unchanging. It rings down through the centuries in splendid isolation, untouched by human hands. A Rock of Ages, no event can budge it from its foundation, no current can deflect it from its course. This solidity brings great comfort to those who embrace it. The virtue of The Rock of Ages is that it was "cleft for me". It provides safety and security to adherents in a world of shifting values. For those who have chosen a permanent truth to dominate their lives the burden of needing to make further choices has been lifted from their shoulders. In exchange they undertake "a service which is perfect freedom"; but this indenture just gives them a feeling of freedom from anxiety in a world where all their decisions have been made for them. One is reminded of Karl Marx's aphorism

"Religion is the opiate of the people."

Their world becomes a well-run insane asylum where all their needs are met. They are cared for by white-robed attendants with a liberal supply of prescriptions to ensure their continued happiness.

Choosing What Is True

A permanent truth is eternal, nothing can change it, but it is not infinite, it has its limitations. Necessarily so, because there are any number of other truths that are just as absolute, just as compelling, perhaps 4,200 of them, all jostling for preferment. A limitation of the domination of a permanent truth over our lives is the fact that we have chosen that particular absolute and permanent truth to be absolutely and permanently true, but there is still part of us that has existence outside of that truth. We can attempt to cut off that part of us, and some do. Perhaps that is what is meant by "becoming a eunuch for God". But who is holding the knife?

Mathematician Kurt Gödel, in his 1931 Theorem of Incompleteness, deduced that a complete description of a system cannot be contained within that system. The system would need to be expanded to contain the complete description of itself, and the expanded system would then need a new description to say it has been expanded to contain a description of itself, and that new description lies outside the system. This means that we have the ability to be self-regarding. It means that part of us will always be outside the system, always able to consider what we regard to be "us" by being outside of us. Thus we will always have the possibility of a role in deciding our affairs even if we have attempted to abandon that responsibility by deferring to a permanent truth. Even though that absolute truth could forbid it, that part of us that chose that truth continues to lie beyond the orbit of such a truth. Events may cause that part of us to be so overtaken by events it may cease to remain dormant and give rise to the need to make another choice, to choose a different truth. The death of a loved one is an event that may provoke such a crisis. If we are convinced that the loved one has gone on to a better place we should be pleased at their good luck, just as we would be pleased if they had just won an all-expense-paid vacation on a cruise ship. Instead we are sorrowful. The feelings of abandonment, of an ending, are stronger than the fears that led us to accept the doctrine of an afterlife. This is particularly true for those who have lost a child. We should be delighted that the little one has gone straight to Heaven without having to put up with all the trials of life, but instead we are inconsolable. Not only do we have a profound sense of loss, we have the feeling of dismay at the disruption of a natural order which decrees that parents should not out-live their children.

To cope, some people indulge in compulsive behavior: to set up a memorial charity, to make a donation to support an institution, to build a monument, to set up a floral display, to write a book, to keep Johnny's room just like it always was, or to seek anaesthesia by any of the medications available. The world is not the same. Its foundation of permanent truth has been shaken, and there is no remedy. The comfort promised by submitting to an absolute truth has proved to be illusory. Some may attempt to recover that comfort by an increasing fanaticism, and some may abandon that truth altogether. There are limits to the hold of a permanent truth: some permanent beliefs might not be held permanently.

Knowing and/or Believing

If I ask somebody "What time is it?" and he looks at his watch and says "It's ten after three" (or "ten past three" in the U.K.) I then know, within a five minute margin of error that the time is somewhere between 15:05 and 15:15. (that's in the afternoon—I don't talk to strangers at 3:00 a.m. in the middle of the night). If I want a more accurate answer I can go to the BBC International Time Signal for the message "at the beginning of the long dash following ten seconds of silence the time will be 21:15 hours Greenwich Mean Time." This gives me useful information. If however when I ask somebody "What time is it?" and he looks at his watch and says "I believe it's ten after three" I am left in doubt. Perhaps his watch or his eyesight is unreliable, perhaps his battery is low, perhaps his watch is stopped altogether, or perhaps he remembers hearing the chimes from Soldiers' Tower a short while ago. His personal assessment has made the time of day a belief with which the rest of the world may not agree. Perhaps he mis-read a "5" as a "3" so his timing is way off. I am looking for a broad consensus of the state of temporal progression so I can organize my affairs to be compatible with those of the rest of the world, and he is offering me a personal belief which might be his alone.

Belief exists on a substrate of doubt. That is why beliefs are held with such passion. Their fragile nature demands our vigorous support to sustain their existence. This is particularly true of religious beliefs, where vindication is particularly tenuous and there are many alternate beliefs clamoring for acceptance.

NOTES for Chapter Three

[15] The Proslogion: a Discourse on the Existence of God, 1078.
[16] Augustine of Hippo, Tractates on the Gospel of John §44 (trans. John W. Rettig), 1995, Catholic University of America Press.
[17] Lewis Carroll (Charles Dodgson), Alice's Adventures in Wonderland and Through the Looking-Glass. 1865.
[18] Kenneth Shouler, The Everything World's Religions Book: 2010, Adams Media, Avon MA
[19] "Beati qui non viderunt, et firmiter crediderunt; vitam aeternam habeunt, Alleluia."
[20] The Five Gospels, the Search for the Authentic Words of Jesus (see 'Distinctive Discourse p 30), Funk and Hoover and The Jesus Seminar, 1993, Macmillan.
[21] The NIV Study Bible, 1995, Zondervan.
[22] Matthew 21: 28
[23] Martin Johnson, Science and the Meaning of Truth, 1946, Isis, London.

CHAPTER FOUR
Three Cosmic FAQ's

All religions offer answers to three leading questions.
        Question No.1 : Where do we come from?
        Question No.2 : Why are we here?
        Question No.3 : Where are we going?

Richard Dawkins writes: "I am very seriously interested in these sorts of questions that 500 years ago would have been given religious answers. In a way I think religion is to be admired for asking the right questions, I just think it's got the wrong answers." These are the three Leading Questions because they are considered the most important questions that can be asked. They relate man to the cosmos. Some people of faith consider these questions to be so important and their answers to them to be so correct they will inflict their answers on us even if we have not asked the question. Some will deal harshly with us[24] to correct us if we dare to question the correctness of their answers. Their answers are so correct, so complete, and so cosmic they are beyond questioning. The problem is: different leaders have different answers to these leading questions, each insisting that his answer is the leading answer.

These questions are also leading questions in the legal sense, because embedded in each of them is a statement. The most famous leading question is "Have you stopped beating your wife yet?" Whatever direct answer you give to such a question is an admission of guilt.

Another example, this time from "The Simpsons" . . .

Homer: "Apu, will you ever stop selling spoiled meat?"
Apu: "No. I mean, yes . . . I mean, oh dear."

In courts of law it is generally the case that leading questions are not allowed while a witness is being directly examined, although they are permitted on cross-examination. Leading questions allow an attorney to suggest the answers he would hope to hear before asking the question. It is a technique that has confused many.

Another feature which applies particularly to these three frequently asked questions is that they are answered much more frequently than they are asked. I cannot recall that I have ever asked any of these questions, and yet total strangers arrive at my door offering their answers. The only themes on television that offer more certainty than these answers are the commercials. The primary sources quoted in church are at best secondary. Luckily, the chapel at Trinity College where I teach has such terrible acoustics for the spoken word that if I avoid sitting in the first eight rows of pews the sermon gets lost in the echo and I am not able to pick out a single word of it, except Amen. I'm not there to have my behavior adjusted or my unbeliefs corrected. Perhaps that is why it is traditional for Anglicans to sit at the back, to avoid the onslaught of unsolicited insights. Hereinafter "FAQ" will indicate "frequently answered questions".

Cosmic FAQ No.1: Where Do We Come From?

Here follows an analysis of how the technique of leading questions has been applied: The first leading question is "Where do we come from?" This is a leading question because it assumes there is/was a "somewhere" from which a "we" came. The question assumes that somewhere there is a place that existed before places were created, a time before time began, where humanity was created before there were any humans. This "we" unites the questioner with the person being questioned, it bundles together all of humanity. Answers to questions of this sort relate to the origin of the universe, to the beginning of time, to the creation of man. If one does not accept these premises the question cannot be answered.

For thousands of years people believed that the creation of man was a special event requiring that a whole day of creation be allocated to the task. Nowadays most people accept a gradual evolution as the most probable provenance for humankind, but a notion inherited from a previous age continues in that we regard humankind as somehow special, that the world exists to serve us, that the purpose of the ostrich is to provide us with feather dusters. We continue to accept as a divine right our domination over the world and all that is in it, and we even assume rights to destroy parts of the world if that would temporarily advance our economies.

I remember how one day, many years ago, I had an experience which led me to see things differently. I was on a voyage from Southampton to New York on the Île de France, my first visit to North America. The weather was terrible—the North Atlantic is not the pleasantest place to be in mid-September, but one day when we were in the middle of the Atlantic we had a day when the weather was wonderful. I went up on deck and as far as the eye could see dolphins were leaping out of the water, thousands and thousands of them in the brilliant sunshine. They were keeping up with our ship, swimming along with us, somersaulting out of the water and diving back under the surface for the pure joy of it, thousands and thousands of them, a huge corps de ballet. They were happy to have our company, and they kept up with us hour after hour. What a wonderful life. Every day they get to go swimming, they go fishing, they feed, they click and sing to one another, they dance, and they make little dolphins. They live in community. They have happy and contented lives, and they have no enemies—except man. This has to be an example of a higher form of life, putting to shame our self-glorifying aspirations, our selfishness. In comparison with the world of the dolphins our world is full of suffering and conflict, our lives marred by anger, anxiety and fear.

Do dolphins have a God? If they needed one it would certainly not be an old man with a beard, part of a failed and unsustainable evolutionary outcome. Possibly they would choose a great whale, a creature descended, like them, from *ambulocetus,* a land animal that millions of years ago had the sense to defy gravity by returning to the sea where life began. Whales still have in their skeletons the vestigial limbs they inherited from when they were a land animal. One branch of descendents of *ambulocetus* remained on land, evolving into the hippopotamus which became a sacred animal to the Egyptians.

Creating the Creator

Religions have no difficulty in offering answers to this leading question "Where do we come from?" The problem is that each religion has its own answer which it holds to be the only true answer. Do we have to pick one of these creation myths as the best possible version of the truth?

The first book in the Hebrew scriptures, the Book of Genesis, begins with the phrase "In the beginning God created the Heavens and the Earth". It is given first place in the Torah because it gives an account of the beginning of the world but it is unlikely that it was the first to be written because it has such a polished literary style and structure. The more rough-and-ready book of Exodus probably preceded it. Genesis, by contrast, consists of ten books, each commencing with the same initial, the first five dealing with creation and the second five with politics. The book has been attributed to

Moses but it is unlikely that he was the author. Moses was formerly an Egyptian and the Egyptian language would have been his native tongue, so it is unlikely that he could create a work of such elegance. If he could write at all it would probably be in hieroglyphics. Genesis bears all the hallmarks of a highly-structured work by a literary scholar.

Genesis depicts a universal god that would be unknown to the early Hebrew people. For them, Yahweh was a tribal god, leading them in battles against their neighbors: the Analects, the Canaanites, the Amorites and the Indianites. Jewish people of that time would regard it as a bizarre concept that the god of their tribe could have created the lands of other tribes. Yahweh himself justified his behavior by claiming that he was a jealous god. The concept of the god mentioned in Genesis, the creator of all, would have been totally alien to them. You can almost hear their argument "If God created the world for us what are all those other people doing here?"

In the beginning God was not the god of the beginning, he was a military attaché seconded to a tribe of nomadic sheep herders. Reports have been received to the effect that he guided the tribesmen through a number of successful campaigns and they established control of a generous territory. Then, like many other military hierarchies, he took on political power and imposed a regime that demanded absolute obedience from his followers. At this point he was mythologized by his followers and credited with creating not only the lands he had conquered but the rest of the universe and everything in it. To be fair, he never claimed that role for himself, he let his followers claim it for him. He gathered all the credit for creating the universe without necessarily having to do it.

Other peoples created their own creation myths; there were thousands of them co-existing. The most bizarre must be that of the earth being a flat disk supported by four elephants standing on the back of a giant turtle swimming in a sea of milk. For thousands of years these myths existed as hypotheses for creation and, without any scientific data to support or oppose any of them, all were equally valid. There was little to choose between them. At that time there was no conflict between scripture and the primitive state of scientific observation.

The first fissure in this cohesive world-view appeared in 230 B.C., when Eratosthenes (276 B.C.—194 B.C.), the Chief Librarian at Alexandria, proposed that the earth was a sphere, and by measuring solar angles at locations separated by great distances he calculated the earth's actual curvature and arrived at a diameter that was accurate to within one percent of present values. The Canadian Flat Earth Society still disputes his findings.

At the same time Aristarchus of Samos (310 B.C.— 230 B.C.), introduced a new idea into cosmology: that the sun is a central fixed point with the earth revolving around it; and the stars could be other bodies like the sun. There was not much support for this view as the geocentric theories based on the philosophy of Aristotle and the astronomy of Ptolemy had had such a widespread acceptance which lasted for over two thousand years.

It was in 1543 that Nicolas Copernicus (1473 – 1543), a Polish mathematician and astronomer, published his book "De revolutionibus orbium coelestium" (On the Revolutions of the Celestial Spheres) which advanced the view that the Earth was in daily motion about its axis and in yearly motion around a stationary sun. This concept was later supported by Giordano Bruno and Galileo Galilei.

Giordano Bruno (1548 – 1600) was a Dominican friar, philosopher, mathematician, astrologer and poet. He supported the concept of Copernicus that the stars could be distant suns surrounded by their own planets. He also postulated an infinite universe and noted that such a universe, being infinite, could not have a centre. This brought him to the attention of the authorities. He was arrested in 1592 and tried by the Inquisition. Most of the charges against him were related to matters of doctrine, but his assertion that there could be multiple worlds was also contrary to the church's teaching. In 1600 he was declared a heretic by Pope Clement VIII, and was burned at the stake the same year.

Ten years later, in 1610, Galileo Galilei published his "Sidereus Nuncius" which recorded observations he had made with his telescope. His instrument had 8X magnification—about the same as modern binoculars—but with it he was able to view the moons of Jupiter. In his honor the four largest moons have now become known as the "Galilean Moons of Jupiter". These were seen to be circulating round their planet, demonstrating that all heavenly bodies were not obliged to circulate around the same single fixed centre. These observations supported the heliocentric theories of Copernicus.

In 1616 the Inquisition declared these views to be heretical, and in 1633 Galileo was brought to trial where he was found to be "gravely suspect of heresy". Pope Paul V ordered him "to abandon all Copernican opinions and to abstain completely from teaching or defending this doctrine and opinion or from discussing it... to abandon it completely... [and hold] the opinion that the sun stands still at the centre of the world and the earth moves, and henceforth not to hold, teach, or defend it in any way whatever, either orally or in writing." Galileo was sentenced to house arrest for the rest of his life. He died in 1642.

Not all the criticism of Copernicus' heliocentric theory came from the Catholic Church. Martin Luther had objections on scriptural grounds. The Book of Joshua 10:13 records that

Joshua, when fighting the battles of the Lord, prayed fervently that the Almighty would continue the light of day that he might complete the slaughter of his enemies[25], saying

"O sun stand still over Gibeon,
O moon over the Valley of Aijalon.
So the sun stood still, and the moon stopped,
till the nation avenged itself on its enemies."

Good for Joshua!—not so great for the Amorites who would not appreciate Joshua's role in extending Daylight Saving Time by stopping the sun in its tracks so he could complete his grisly purpose. This event is celebrated in the rituals of Freemasonry as evidence for the efficacy of prayer.

It is unfortunate that these conflicting interpretations of phenomena are expressed in absolute terms when they are so dependent on the position of the observer. From the point of view of an observer on earth it is clear that the sun revolves around the earth— we talk about sunrise, not earth-fall. From the point of view of the solar system the earth moves around the sun together with the rest of the planets—and for a visitor from outer space the whole thing is rotating with the galaxy. All of you are right— now can we stop killing one another?

In 1891, in a measure of "catch up", Pope Leo XIII established the Vatican Observatory, based in Tucson Arizona. The purpose was to show that "the Church and her Pastors are not opposed to true and solid science, whether human or divine". The present Director of the Observatory, Rev. José G. Funes S.J., considering the possibility of extra-terrestrial life, stated in an interview:

"Scientists believe that by comparing our own planets atmosphere to those of planets outside our solar system, they can get closer to understanding the possibility of life on other planets. These planets have atmospheres that can be similar to the atmosphere on earth and have what we call biomarkers so those elements give help to the development of life."

This statement still continues the tribal mind-set that life is only to be found in water-based oxygen-breathing beings like us, and that we are images of God. It brings up such theological questions as

> "Did Christ also die for the sins of germanium-based electrical-impulse-energized beings floating around on distant planets?".
>
> "Could there be a vacancy for new members at the Holy Trinity."
>
> "Could the Father also adopt or download a cyber-Son?"

Luckily atheists do not have to be troubled by such conjectures.

On being asked whether he believed in the possibility of intelligent life on other planets Sir James Jeans, the British Astronomer-Royal, after considering the myriads of planets surrounding billions of stars, replied "Not only do I consider intelligent life on other planets a possibility, I believe that somewhere, out there, there is a cricket team capable of beating the Australians."

In 1992, the Catholic Church under Pope John Paul II finally repealed the 1642 ruling of the Inquisition against Galileo, giving him a pardon and admitting that the heliocentric theory was correct. Bruno is still awaiting restitution.

We have seen how, through the ages, statements made about the world have been proclaimed as absolute truth. As knowledge developed some of these statements needed to be modified, requiring a change of absolute truths. At each revision there were some who did not go along with the changes. Some dropped off when it was proclaimed that the Bible was inerrant but not necessarily infallible. More abandoned the mainstream when most people accepted the concept of Evolution. The Creationists, those left behind, are fighting difficult rearguard actions. The Creation Museum in Petersburg, Kentucky, has exhibits of pieces of fossilized shale showing what are alleged to be human and dinosaur footprints together. This is presented as proof that humans and dinosaurs co-existed. The prints, of both sorts are flat, not the imprints of feet that are running away. These must be the footprints of a human taking his pet dinosaur for a walk.

Canada has its own Creation Science Museum at Big Valley, Alberta. It's on a smaller scale than the museum in Kentucky which cost $28 million. Against that, the scaled down Canadian version cost a modest one-hundredth of that amount. The museum traces the ancestry of the British Royal Family back to Adam and Eve, and presents fossils as evidence for the flood of Noah. These museums are attempts to make reality correspond to writings. As time rolls by the discrepancies between the two multiplied and the task became more and more difficult, but there appears to be a limitless supply of energy for the task, springing from the need to relate a creator-god to a physical reality that is always changing.

In an effort to hold things together Pope Pius X attempted to staunch the flow with his 1907 encyclical "Pascendi Dominici Gregis", (Feeding the Lord's Flock), in which he condemned Modernism and Evolutionary Principles, and the heresies behind them. Modernism was a name created in the Vatican to include various dangerous "novelties".

In 1910, to cleanse from the priesthood theologians promoting Modernism he issued "The Oath Against Modernism", requiring that it be sworn to by all clergy, pastors, confessors, preachers, religious superiors, and professors in philosophical-theological seminaries (which would have included me). Here follows the text, ready for signature:

THE OATH AGAINST MODERNISM

"I. . . . . firmly embrace and accept each and every definition that has been set forth and declared by the unerring teaching authority of the Church, especially those principal truths which are directly opposed to the errors of this day. First of all, I profess that God, the origin and end of all things, can be known with certainty by the natural light of reason from the created world (see Rom. 1:19), that is, from the visible works of creation, as a cause from its effects, and that, therefore, his existence can also be demonstrated:

"Secondly, I accept and acknowledge the external proofs of revelation, that is, divine acts and especially miracles and prophecies as the surest signs of the divine origin of the Christian religion and I hold that these same proofs are well adapted to the understanding of all eras and all men, even of this time.

"Thirdly, I believe with equally firm faith that the Church, the guardian and teacher of the revealed word, was personally instituted by the real and historical Christ when he lived among us, and that the Church was built upon Peter, the prince of the apostolic hierarchy, and his successors for the duration of time.

"Fourthly, I sincerely hold that the doctrine of faith was handed down to us from the apostles through the orthodox Fathers in exactly the same meaning and always in the same purport. Therefore, I entirely reject the heretical misrepresentation that dogmas evolve and change from one meaning to another different from the one which the Church held previously. I also condemn every error according to which, in place of the divine deposit which has been given to the spouse of Christ to be carefully guarded by her, there is put a philosophical figment or product of a human conscience that has gradually been developed by human effort and will continue to develop indefinitely.

"Furthermore, I reject the opinion of those who hold that a professor lecturing or writing on a historico-theological subject should first put aside any preconceived opinion about the supernatural origin of Catholic tradition or about the divine promise of help to preserve all revealed truth forever; and that they should then interpret the writings of each of the Fathers solely by scientific principles, excluding all sacred authority, and with the same liberty of judgment that is common in the investigation of all ordinary historical documents.

"Finally, I declare that I am completely opposed to the error of the modernists who hold that there is nothing divine in sacred tradition; or what is far worse, say that there is, but in a pantheistic sense, with the result that there would remain nothing but this plain simple fact—one to be put on a par with the ordinary facts of history—the fact, namely, that a group of men by their own labor, skill, and talent have continued through subsequent ages a school begun by Christ and his apostles. I firmly hold, then, and shall hold to my dying breath the belief of the Fathers in the charism of truth, which certainly is, was, and always will be in the succession of the episcopacy from the apostles. The purpose of this is, then, not that dogma may be tailored according to what seems better and more suited to the culture of each age; rather, that the absolute and immutable truth preached by the apostles from the beginning may never be believed to be different, may never be understood in any other way.

"I promise that I shall keep all these articles faithfully, entirely, and sincerely, and guard them inviolate, in no way deviating from them in teaching or in any way in word or in writing. Thus I promise, this I swear, so help me God"

Signed..................

This draconian edict remained in force for sixty years. During that time 'Councils of Vigilance' were set up and scholarship was to be censored, usually by people of lesser intellect than the authors. Bishops were given authority to prevent the publication of modernist works, to investigate catholic booksellers, and drive any pernicious books, such as this one, out of their dioceses. It was not until 1967 that Pope Paul VI ended this assault on freedom by abolishing the Oath for priests.

A similar restriction of deviant thought was imposed on the 160 employees of the Museum of Creation in Kentucky by its management: the "Answers in Genesis" group. Each permanent employee must sign a statement of faith indicating that he or she believes in the teachings of Answers in Genesis. These include:

"Scripture teaches a recent origin for man and the whole creation,

"The only legitimate marriage is the joining of one man and one woman,

"The great Flood of Noah was an actual historic event, and

"No perceived or claimed evidence in any field can be valid if it contradicts the Scriptural record"

This discriminatory requirement, that members of staff should have an acceptable belief system as a condition of engagement made the museum ineligible for public funding.

Application Form

Applications are invited for the position of God.

While adhering strictly to a policy of non-discrimination, preference will be given to those applicants who are white, male, bearded, of mature years and under the tongue of good report.

The duties and responsibilities of the position are as follows

1. To create the Heavens and the Earth
2. To create Man in God's image (for conformity a retroactive template will be provided)
3. To create Woman in Man's image (some internal modifications may be required)
4. To choose the Chosen People.
5. To lay down the Law on the Chosen People.
6. To smite mightily the enemies of the Chosen People with plagues, floods, quakes, conflagrations, and the sword.
7. To smite mightily the Chosen People when they step out of line.
8. To make your Chosen People grateful.
9. To maintain an inbox for intercessions.
10. To be our guide and keeper, defending our eyes from ghostly feares & fantasies.
11. To preside over Heaven, seated on the throne of heavenly grace.
12. To be the judge of all men, rewarding virtue and punishing vice.

Remuneration will consist of everlasting praise and glory, for which eternal choirs will sing the praises of the successful candidate, with accompaniment by harpists in Heaven, and on Earth organists.

Fig. 4. Typical Application Form

All people of faith believed that their world was created by god, but first they had to be sure that their god would be suitable for the role—a typical application form is illustrated in Fig. 4. It's obvious that people create gods, because their gods so closely resemble the people they are engaged to create[26]. This correspondence indicates that before a god is allowed to create people in his own image he himself has to be created in the people's image. This is celebrated in the song "Togetherness"[27], where Anglicans assert their core belief that:

"God is a gentleman
    Through and through,
And He is most probably Anglican too."

God's creation of man is a simple linear progression, it's not a recursive feed-back loop. It's not a chicken-and-egg situation. (Neither, according to physicist Robert Logan, is the chicken and egg progression. The egg came first. The chicken is just the egg's way of making another egg.) This progression was noted in Winston Churchill's aphorism[28] on the rebuilding of the House of Commons after it had been destroyed in the war "We shape our buildings, and afterwards our buildings shape us."

"Creator of the Universe" is both the easiest and the most difficult role for people of faith to ascribe to god. Easiest, because as an end-product we have the reality of the physical world as proof of the process—difficult because that reality keeps changing, so there is a continual need to edit the evidence. However, we should be aware that in spite of whatever answers we may give to the question "Who (or what) created the heavens and the earth" it is still a leading question. Embedded in it is the assumption that the world was created by some agency, and this agency, of necessity, had to exist outside the world and before the world existed, a deus-ex-machina. This is an extension of our every-day logic and experience. If we see a loaf of bread we can assume the existence of a baker. Breads and bakers both exist in our experiences in our every-day world and we are aware of the relationship that exists between them. However, there are difficulties in extrapolating these relationships into realms of the very large or the very small. At very large scales, such as that of the universe, Einstein's General Theory of Relativity complicates our simple rules of arithmetic. At very small scales, such as the inception of the origin of the universe, Quantum Theory offers multiple possible answers to a simple enquiry of cause and effect. Bakers might formulate breads, but their recipes would be useless if there were no ovens. Dough has no form, and all the designing in the world would not transform it into loaves if there were no ovens to bake it. The oven creates a heated space, a high-energy environment, that transforms dough into bread. Large commercial bakeries use machines to put the dough in the oven—not a baker in sight.

Does the universe need a baker? A problem that had been troubling mathematicians and cosmologists for a long time is that the universe contains lots of stuff, sometimes in massive amounts, but where did this mass come from? When a new particle is created it travels at the speed of light, and the Theory of Relativity holds that to attain that speed its mass would have to be zero. So what sort of creative process created the mass we see all around us? Where did all this mass come from? In 1964 Peter Higgs and five others discovered in a mathematical relationship a possibility that would permit the existence of a particle whose speed would be less that the speed of light, and that reduced speed would allow it to have a positive mass. This theoretical particle was named the Higgs boson after Peter Higgs. At that time the only evidence for it was a single page of mathematical equations indicating a theoretical possibility.

According to quantum-field theory every field has an associated quantum particle, so if the Higgs boson exists there would have to be a Higgs field with which the Higgs boson is associated. This field would be an energy field that exists everywhere in the universe and fills all space. The field uses its particle, the Higgs boson, to interact continuously with other particles. As particles pass through the field they acquire energy from the field. This energy creates a relative mass, so a particle that was formerly without mass slows down because it has become "heavier". The Higgs field, if it exists, could be the mechanism by which particles acquire the mass necessary for them to be able to attract one another, and without such mass they would float around freely as individual particles at the speed of light, and not be able to combine to form either matter or us.

The possibility that the Higgs field could be the agency for creating matter from empty space captured the imagination of scientists everywhere. It would not be possible to verify the existence of the Higgs field directly, but if its associated particle, the Higgs boson, could be detected that would provide evidence of the existence of the field. The boson, too, could not be detected directly, but its presence could be deduced from its interaction with other particles. To force this interaction would require the focus of huge amounts of energy; more than was currently available. However this research was considered so important that work was started in 1988 on a new facility could handle such a high energy level.

This was the Superconducting Super Collider, designed to accelerate proton particles along a circular 87.1 kilometer track in a deep underground tunnel surrounding the town of Waxahachie, Texas. Congress approved a budget for the project of five billion dollars.

With an initial contribution of two billion dollars the first section of the tunnel and it's access shafts were built, but there were problems in securing a second installment of funding and Congress cancelled the project in 1993. The reasons were:

> The project had been proudly described as "an all-American project built in America with American know-how" which made other countries reluctant to contribute any of their expected support.
> Some of the scientists talked down to Congress as if they were ignorant hicks, and they described the project in kilometers rather than miles, and
> The Higgs boson had been named "the God Particle" by Leon Lederman[29], which gave the project popular appeal but in the eyes of many members of Congress made the project redundant because we already had all the answers we would need in the Book of Genesis.

Future generations may puzzle over the function of these vast abandoned tunnels, relic of an earlier civilization. Clearly they would have had, like Stonehenge, some religious significance for those earlier times. In 1998 work was begun on creating a vast accelerator in Europe. This was the Large Hadron Collider operated by the European Organization for Nuclear Research (CERN) with headquarters in Geneva. The project was supported by contributions from over one hundred countries and cost $9 billion. The research facility consists of a circular tunnel with a circumference of 27 kilometers buried 100 meters underground and traversing the French/Swiss border. The laboratory examines collisions between opposing beams of protons, reproducing those conditions that existed within a billionth of a second after the Big Bang 14 billion years ago. Two beams of high-energy protons are accelerated to near the speed of light as they are guided in opposite directions around a 27 km circular path where they are crash into one another. Detectors record the debris from these collisions which are analyzed by a computer network of huge capacity. On 14 March 2013 the collider confirmed that among the traces of particles scattered by the collision a particle had been detected with the fundamental criteria for a Higgs boson, the only fundamental particle with zero spin to be discovered in nature.

Fig. 5 The Large Hadron Collider in Switzerland, operated by CERN.

The detection of the Higgs boson confirmed the existence of the Higgs field and a potential for the creation of matter by space. This relieves God of the necessity of creating the world; the world is perfectly capable of creating itself. God's job, at least in this respect, has been rendered redundant by technology. He can take an early retirement. The universe creates itself.

This is a truly beautiful concept, that everything is created out of nothing. It should humble us to know that we emerged from void and save us from the arrogance of claiming a special and superior ancestry. Compared with the elegance and rigor of this process, all the creation myths, including the story in Genesis, are crude fantasies.

Strangely, this new role that has been verified for space relates to a discovery I made in a course I teach at Trinity College titled "Shaping Space for Worship". The course is designed to enliven congregations by aligning their liturgy, their mission, their focus, the way they gather and the spaces they occupy. As part of the process we attempt to analyze space; and we go some way to defining it by observing the ways in which we describe it. If we take a very high space such as the main hall at Grand Central Station which has an 80-foot ceiling—that space we would describe as leaping, soaring, or flying. Take a low spreading space such as the bottom level of a large underground parking garage, that space we could describe as crushing, oppressing. Take a long narrow space such as the space we see by sitting at the front of a subway train and looking down the tunnel, that space we would describe as stretching, extending. What all these descriptions have in common is that they are all verbs, they all relate to things we can do with our bodies. We can leap and soar and crush and stretch. These are all human capabilities. Of course we are not really stretched and crushed, but at the same time, in a deep basement I feel that crushing weight overhead, and in Grand Central Station I walk on the floor like everybody else while feeling like flying. We describe space in terms of our bodies. We imagine what we would have to do in order to experience what we perceive as the quality of the space, and then we describe the space as if it were itself performing these actions. We describe space by identifying with it, and then looking inside ourselves. It is wonderful that space, the most distant, immaterial quantity we can imagine, is experienced by our bodies, our closest contact with the material world. Space can dance and sing, space can laugh, space can wonder, space can pray, and space can speak to us. Space can worship, which means that space can support our worship, and space is creative. The only thing that objects can do is to be objects, they are nouns; but space being a verb is creative, rich with potential. Space can do things, and one of the things it can do with its creative power is to create the universe. Lawrence Krauss, a cosmologist at Arizona State University[30] commented on this, saying

> "It's beautiful, the fact that empty space is endowed with these properties—that what appears to be empty space endows particles with a mass. Apparently, nothingness is responsible for our existence. The fact that Peter Higgs and five others dreamed this up back in the 1960s is almost as remarkable. Normally, experiment leads theory but in this case, theory ran ahead by half a century."

I too find it an extraordinarily beautiful concept that space can create stuff, that nothing is needed to create a universe, except nothing.

NOTES for Chapter Four

[24] Those who reject faith...they will be companions of the Fire, dwelling therein for ever. (The Holy Quran 3:116)
[25] Donald H. Kobe. Copernicus and Martin Luther –an Encounter between Science and Religion, 1998, American Journal of Physics.
[26] "And it is in his own image, let us remember, that Man creates God." H. Havelock Ellis: Impressions and Comments, July 18. Echo Library 2010.
[27] Spring Thaw Revue, Toronto 1959.
[28] speech in the House of Commons (meeting in the House of Lords), October 28, 1943.
[29] Leon M. Lederman, The God Particle, 1993. Dell Publishing, New York.
[30] Lunau and Engelhart. "Why the Higgs boson discovery changed everything", Maclean's Magazine: July 17, 2012

CHAPTER FIVE

Cosmic FAQ No.2: Why Are We Here?

This question is of little importance. Because our lives are so unsustainable we will not be here for long. If we were part of a divine plan, that plan, for us, contains some fatal flaw and has been very badly executed. Existence is winding down. All we can do in these last days, as we rush towards that tipping point where our extinction becomes inevitable, is to be kind to one another in mutually administered palliative care.

Why are we here? This question could be expressed in two ways—

By what process were we generated?, and

What is the purpose for our existence?

The answer to the first interpretation is easy. Most people accept that humankind evolved from more primitive life-forms. Those who do not accept that view consider that men were created from dust and breath, and women from spareribs. As for children, their creation is equally bizarre:

"What are little girls made of?

Sugar and spice and all things nice

—that's what little girls are made of.

What are little boys made of?

Slugs and snails and puppy-dogs' tails

—that's what little boys are made of."

There is less consensus about the second interpretation "What is the purpose for our existence?" but let's try to answer the question anyway. Why are we here? Buried in the second leading question is the assumption that we are a result of a decision that has been taken, that there is a purpose for us to be here. If there should be no reason for us to be here beyond a series of accidental events the question does not have an answer. Some assert that the fact of our existence is evidence of the will of God acting in a determinist universe. That situation would require the co-existence of God and ourselves. From that view it would follow that we exist to fulfill some divine purpose, that God gives our life meaning. Many who wish to have a life that has meaning adopt a God that will define a suitable meaning and purpose for their lives.

Atheists know that we exist and God doesn't, so for atheists there is no divine purpose for our lives. Any purpose we accept for ourselves results from our individual choice. Life is essentially meaningless. Seeking "The Meaning of Life" is the quest for an illusion. To realize that life is meaningless is such a blessing (if I may be permitted to use that word). It allows us to choose for our lives whatever purpose pleases us. Life becomes a game, to be played just for the sheer enjoyment of its exciting possibilities.

Life is a game; sometimes a multi-player game, with rules, strategies, a scoring system, rewards and penalties, prizes, and a time limit. It may be played on several levels at the same time. The game is both competitive and co-operative. It is available to individual players and also to partnerships and teams. Some teams may wish to signal their community of purpose by wearing distinctive uniforms, by holding up flags and banners with symbols and slogans, by performing rituals celebrating their own songs and stories, and perhaps employing coaches to maintain direction, and team captains to maintain order.

Life is a game of both skill and chance, to be played with grace and style. Lord Shiva[31] presents life as a dance, a ring of fire depicting its energy and his six-limbed poise expressing its grace.

And life must be fun. That is essential. For me it is fun to be writing this outrageous book, one of the most serious tasks I have ever undertaken. My hope is that it will bring you comfort and joy and perhaps entertainment—for me that

Fig. 6. Shiva Nataraja—The Eternal Dance

would constitute a "Win"; but there is always the chance that before the game I am playing is completed and last page is written the beeper will go off, signalling "Timed Out!".

Atheists have more fun than do people of faith. Life is a comedy for those who think, and a tragedy for those who feel. To check that statement read a passage from any book on religion and check whether this book isn't more fun. Atheists choose the games they choose to play, and they play them only while the fun lasts, and they are always free to choose another game, or play two games at the same time. Right now I am playing two games at the same time. In one game I teach students who wish to become ministers of religion, in the other game I am writing this book to promote the joys of atheism. I leave you with a game to play; a puzzle: am I promoting atheism, or am I promoting faith by offering, like Pascal, counter arguments to religious beliefs that are so easily refutable?

Games have rules. Atheists adopt whatever rules serve them, whatever rules make the game exciting, and they can change the rules or change the game if they wish. People of faith do not have that freedom. One of the rules of their game is that they cannot change the rules (because they are the right rules) and they may not leave the game (because it is the right game). If they leave the game they have lost. It is said of those who choose to no longer play the authorized game that they have lost their faith; as if by an increase in their freedoms they have lost something.

That is sad. Some mourn their loss; but it is considered more reprehensible if the player decides not just to quit playing but to start playing a different game, one of the many wrong games. Some games have rules that require strong measures to be taken against those who persist in playing an illicit game. Some who insist on persisting in their error in the face of extreme efforts to persuade them to adopt the contrary opinion may later join the noble company of martyrs, with their images sanctified in stained glass.

For the rest of us, we are given a time on earth that we can spend as best we can. This is expressed quite beautifully in The Russian Kontakion for the Dead:

"O Glorious God
Thou only art immortal,
The Creator and Maker of man:
And we are mortal,

formed of the earth,
and unto earth we shall return:
For so thou didst ordain,
When thou createdest me, saying
'Dust thou art, and unto dust shalt thou return.'
All we go down to the dust,
    and, weeping o'er the grave,
    we make our song: rejoicing
        Alleluya, Alleluya, Alleluya."

From molecules found in a pile of dust ejected from exploding stars I was created; molecules that combined, reacted, polymerized to create calcium-based compounds to form the skeletal structure of my hands, and organic molecules to sheathe them with connective tissue. These boney structures are now pressing down on the keys of a keyboard, each key bearing a letter they don't need to look at, they know where they are, and this pressure releases electrical impulses that create light-and-dark images on the page of a book which a pressure from the skeleton of your hands is holding up, so differential reflections from the printed page can enter your eyes and stimulate the retinal evagination of the brain so your mind can receive a message from my mind.

It's always a bit sad when something ends, but the grave is just a receptacle for discarded dust waiting to be recycled, and I rejoice that the purpose I have chosen for my life can live on after my life is over; that this song can continue to be heard. The possibility of that is sufficient

Happy Accident or Intelligent Design?

I have been an architect for many years, and I have come to realize that most designing involves the rejection of options. It is only after many options have been considered that the most acceptable one appears, and once it has been identified it becomes obvious that that was the best solution all along. Rejecting options is a rational process, but accepting the ultimate solution is not rational at all, it comes in a blinding flash. Out of a near-infinite array of options the solution is often recognized before it is understood. Piet Hein[32], a Danish mathematician and poet said "A work of art is the answer to a question, but that question can only be asked after we have the answer. The question is implicit in the work; it is not explicit." I find a well crafted design answers so many questions simultaneously that I can never pick out which one is the "right" one. If a client asks me "Why did you do that?" I can't give an answer—all I can say is "just look at the solution! It's obvious it's the right one, solving all sorts of problems we did not know we had. It will answer questions you have not even asked yet." These solutions are strange and unexpected and yet they appear to be intimately familiar. Even though the design appears inevitable I can never give a convincing reason for it in retrospect.

In the world of nature it is very clear what options have been rejected—they did not survive. This does not mean that the environment was crafted to encourage the survival of any particular species, the environment evolved as it did, and whatever species could survive in that environment did so, the rest were taken off the board. It's difficult to see the need for any external intelligence to decree how the environment should be; it's doing very well on its own. The environment is a work in progress, subject to constant change. It's erratic trajectory is not consistent with the fulfillment of any master plan. There appears to be no plan, so it's hard to imagine a planner who would deliberately guide the world along such a tortuous path with back-ups and reversals and dead ends; and it's hard to see any purpose for what has been allowed to survive. If in fact there is a design it's not a very intelligent one.

In architectural design the rejection of options becomes particularly obvious when choosing the paint colors for a room. Paint manufacturers produce multi-hued catalogues with thousands of options, and from this vast listing of possibilities there is just one survivor—survival of the prettiest. Paint colors became an issue in the 1980's when I was designing a waterfront development at Point Edward, Ontario, on the shores of the St. Clair River. I had noticed that on waterfronts in such places as Peggy's Cove in the Maritimes the houses were painted in bright colors but the result was harmonious; not at all garish. To recreate this nautical flavor and honor a Canadian tradition I chose as a discipline to use only colors that had been available in the 1600's, which was the way the original houses would have been painted. I identified a dozen colors with wonderful names like ochre, cinnabar, orpiment, and rose-madder. The result was a joyful clash of colorations, as if all the later formulations of the chemical industry had, like the dinosaurs, become extinct and the surviving colors were united by a commonality.

We were surrounded by colors when returning from a brief canoe trip on Naiscoot Lake with my friend Ranjan. It was early evening as we paddled back across the lake to the cabin where our supper would be waiting for us. The golden orb of the sun behind us was painting the sky with flame as it sank below the horizon while in front of us tufts of cumulus were tinged with ultramarine, cerulean, and violet against a darkening sky. It was that time of calm at near-dusk when the wind shifts from a lake breeze to a land breeze. The lake was as clear as a mirror, reflecting beneath us the same rich melding of colors as of the sky above us so it was as if we were suspended at the centre of a sphere of multi-colored glass, the upper and lower hemispheres separated by a narrow band of rock and tree. It was absolutely quiet, the silence broken only by the drip from our paddles and the call of a loon, with a faint echo from another, perhaps his mate, in the next lake. Moved by such beauty, Ranjan said "How can people say there is no God?"

True such a wonderful harmony of elements would be beyond the design capability of any human. With respect I would say it would also be beyond the capability of any God. What created this concordance? There are many factors:

> The apparent setting of the sun resulted from the rotation of the Earth on its axis.
> The pink, orange, red colorations resulted from the increase in the preferential scattering of the higher (blue) frequencies due to the increased path-length through the atmosphere when the elevation is near-tangential.
> The clouds resulted from the condensation of water vapor in the atmosphere to create masses of visible water droplets and ice crystals.
> The blue sky beyond the clouds resulted from the scattered higher frequencies of (blue) light masking the black sky of outer space.
> The water resulted from hydrogen molecules which had condensed from the after-effects of the Big Bang being bombarded by oxygen from within the sun.
> The channel resulted from gouging by a 2 km thick sheet of ice set in motion by the melting of the glaciers 70,000 years ago.
> The rock resulted from volcanic magma slowly cooling into a crystalline structure over millions of years.
> The calm resulted from a null point when the direction of the wind was about to change due to a reversing temperature gradient as the land cooled faster than the water.

The loon resulted from an evolutionary opportunity for a fish-eating bird that could be equally competent swimming underwater or flying through the air: they can dive to 200 feet, and fly at 120 kph.

And the most unlikely outcome of all—that Ranjan (from Sri Lanka) and myself (from the U.K.) should find ourselves on a September evening paddling a canoe across a Canadian lake.

Did somebody design this wonderful harmony? Design has a purpose—was the purpose for all this overarching beauty to provide an enjoyable aesthetic experience for Ranjan and myself on a September evening? Is that the meaning of the universe? Somehow, I doubt it. This beauty could not have appeared at a single stroke. It was the survivor of a million million million accidents. Perhaps it represents the balance between a million opposing forces—boiling granite solidifying into the Pre-Cambrian Shield, water gathering into a rift created by glaciers 70,000 years ago, the calibration of the fading light as our planet rotates its face away from its sun, silences between the sounds of nature. This cascade of events must have been a series of happy accidents. Evidence for that statement is that the changes are still happening. I'm writing this in December. Now the lake is frozen and bears an overburden of snow. The loons have migrated south to find more open water. What we experienced was a snapshot of an ever-changing evolving scene. A design to fulfill a purpose is not a death but it represents a completion, an ending of a process, a finality, while an evolution is open-ended, messy, surprising, unpredictable, inconsistent and impermanent. These are the hallmarks of a system that evolved without the involvement of a designer, and those are characteristics of our universe.

I had to confront this situation many years ago, when as a young architect I was commissioned to design The

Colonnade, a multi-use building on Toronto's fashionable Bloor Street with stores, offices, apartments and a theatre. At that time apartment towers were starting to spring up in the outlying areas surrounding the city, and with a few exceptions they all looked the same. There was not much to choose between them. They all had an exposed concrete frame with infill panels of glazed brick, concrete balconies, and floor-to-ceiling glass. To make sure that they would all have a uniform appearance the only permitted window covering was roll-up blinds of matchstick-bamboo. That was written into all the apartment leases. The result was that all the windows of all the apartment buildings right across the City were beige. That design decision ended the hope for any sort of personal expression or creativity. The buildings where people lived had to look like nobody lived there.

When we started working on The Colonnade we wanted to attract people who had fled to the suburbs; we wanted them to come back to the city, so the building should have a lively appearance and not look like just another office building, it should be a celebration of urban living. To that end we did not have any restrictive clauses in the apartment leases and people were free to use whatever window covering they wished. However people were so conditioned by previous experience that all the initial tenants opted to install beige bamboo, bearing out Eric Hoffer's aphorism "When people are free to do as they please, they usually imitate each other." In order to give the building an air of human occupancy we had to revise the leases to say that matchstick bamboo was the one form of window covering that would not be permitted—anything else but. We had to abandon the role of overall designers to encourage the interest and variety of individual expressions. Buildings which demand their tenants hide behind beige bamboo present to the world a design that is unchanging, un-human, deadly if not dead; while The

Colonnade presents evidence of an evolution of happy accidents which will continue to evolve into the future. This has obvious parallels with the evolution of the universe.

Fig. 7. The Colonnade welcomes those returning to life in the city.

Some designers attempt to give a building a more human scale by designing a façade that would look like different individuals had designed different bits of it. This is getting to be fairly common in condominium developments where variety is accomplished by having some units pop out and some be recessed, or by having different sorts of cladding in different parts of the building. This attempt to be playful never works. It is not possible to be playful with a hundred tons of concrete. The quick sketch on a napkin requires a huge investment in engineering expertise if it is to be implemented. This sort of design is tyranny: a designer creating a structure without logic where future generations will have to adapt themselves to comply and which they are powerless to alter. There is nothing casual about it. Casual means "without serious intention", yet design is inherently intentional, so a casual design is not possible, and people will be able to tell the difference, just as it's possible for people to perceive the difference between Disneyland and Prague.

This failure is found in all those residential developments that have the word "Village" in their title—none of them feels like a village. They are all too organized, too regular, too logical; and when there is an attempt to inject something outrageous to give relief from all this logic, that too is the result of a logical decision. This troubled me when I undertook the commission to design Venetian Village, a 120 unit waterfront development—how to make a development built in the 1980's look as if it had evolved over several centuries. Besides the discipline of color mentioned above, the answer I came up with was to mimic the evolution process itself. In a "real" village, first a couple of houses spring up. Then a mill is built at a nearby stream and a few more houses appear, one of which becomes the village store. A church arrives, and decently distant from it a public house. Between these two there is space for a row of cottages. They have to fit exactly the available space—it would not be possible to move the church or the pub to achieve a better-designed cottage. It struck me that this was the clue: we would need a design process that mimicked an evolving and irreversible sequence of events. We would have to move continuously forward; forward into a future where there would be no possibility of revising the past, no feedback loops.

To do this we first built a very large model of the land area of the entire site. It filled an entire conference room. Then we made up models of all the units. We knew that for 120 houses we would require 120 living rooms, dining areas, kitchens, together with 300 bedrooms and 240 bathrooms, so we cut blocks of wood to represent these rooms so when they were glued together they would represent houses. Some of these houses we glued to various points on the site model and this became the seed of the development.

Then we started to infill. The rule was: once a piece had been glued down it could not be taken up again or moved, just as you cannot move a church to free up a bit more space for the house next door. This created some interesting

Fig.8. Venetian Village: a settlement formed by accelerated evolution.

problems: when a space between two blocks was too narrow to take a regular house we had to insert a taller house and let the top floor overhang its neighbor. This created exactly the sort of interest you find in an existing village, and we knew that when the last block had been glued in place, when the bag of loose blocks was empty, we would have fulfilled the economic mandate of the developer. When the last block was glued down we carefully measured the arrangement, and that drawing became our site plan. It all worked out fairly well, Venetian Village is obviously not Peggy's Cove, but when you are there you do not sense the presence of an all-powerful designer, perhaps because there wasn't one; and it was ironic that the project received a design award from the Governor General because nobody designed it. Like the universe, it just evolved.

Some people are disturbed by the notion that the universe appears to be launched on a random course with nobody in control. At Expo67 in Montreal the monorail which ferried people around the exposition site was fully automated. It would automatically stop and start at the correct point at every station, but some people were afraid to use it so the management hired a student to sit at the front and wear a peaked cap and look as if he was in control of the situation. In fact, the automatic system worked with far more precision than any human could contribute. In a recent experiment a driverless car drove for eight hours a day a total of 112,000 kilometers without incident, an achievement that a human driver would have difficulty in matching.

The superior performance of automatic systems was noted by Charles Haanel, author of "The Twenty-Four Parts", with reference to the nervous system. He noted that tasks directed by the unconscious mind under the control of the Sympathetic Nervous System are accomplished perfectly and effortlessly, without our knowledge or involvement. These tasks include breathing and the circulation of the blood which are regulated even when we sleep. They also include such learned tasks as language, tying shoelaces and driving a car. Technology has not yet been able to write a program to enable a robot to tie shoelaces, yet many of us are able to accomplish this task without effort or concentration. Tasks which require our conscious attention are directed by the Parasympathetic Nervous System, which also provides information for the Sympathetic Nervous System. When learning to drive a car the parasympathetic system is engaged for information handling and decision making. The would-be driver is hesitant cautious and erratic as the task absorbs all his concentration. ("There's an obstruction up ahead! Should I push on one of those pedals? Which one? Oops!") After practice the sympathetic nervous system absorbs the information and takes over much of the operation and we can relax some of our conscious control, trusting in our automatic reactions. Driving becomes automatic, and thereby safer, with correct responses appearing faster than we can think about them.

Automatic systems are safer and more precise than any we could think into existence. The monorail at Expo ran with more precision and safety than any human could achieve. Venetian Village would not have turned out so well if I had attempted to design it instead of just leaving it up to chance and collecting an architect's fee for a design I didn't do; and it's possible the development of the universe would not have been so magnificent if God had had a hand in it.

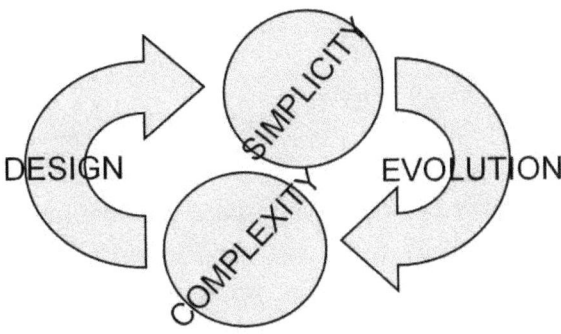

Fig. 9. From design and evolution: opposite outcomes.

If design is a process of eliminating possible options its effect must be to simplify complex situations, to create order out of chaos, to narrow our scope until it crystallizes into a single example of perfection. Evolution is just the opposite, continually offering new experiences, new complications, new opportunities, new life. In a strange role-reversal atheists have faith that the World is self-regulating and is unfolding as it should; while people of faith are inherently distrustful of its ability to manage its own affairs. They do not trust themselves, society, or this wonderful world around us. Essentially they are trapped in a continuation of an infantile dependency, seeking the assurance of some authority figure, even if they have to make one up to fill the bill. Their god is a construct of human weakness. Thus they may refer to their deity as a parent (Father or Mother), or as a powerful member of the aristocracy (Lord or King), or as a custodian dedicated to their welfare (Shepherd or Servant). Many derive great comfort from these beliefs—for them it's just too scary to consider that the Universe might be running out-of-control, doing its own thing which might not be our thing, having a purpose which might not be our purpose, or even more scary —having no purpose at all; but (to quote George Bernard Shaw[33]) "the fact that a believer is happier than a skeptic is no more to the point than the fact that a drunken man is happier than a sober one." What is comforting and what is true are two entirely different things.

However we see much beauty in the Universe. In response to our probing it yields insights of unsurpassing elegance. And while we are enjoying its hospitality our lives are capable of finding fulfillment and experiencing joy. That's a lot, it's really huge. So perhaps we are able, with the otherwise-depressed T.S. Eliot, to "rejoice that things are as they are."[34] (Somehow I can't imagine T.S. Eliot rejoicing, but I'm glad he found joy somewhere).

Design Unpacked

The subject is complicated because we use the same words to describe opposing qualities. Design, as a noun, does not necessarily evolve from the process of designing (as a verb). We use the word "design" as a noun to describe any coherent arrangement of things, but that arrangement did not necessarily come into being because somebody, or Somebody, designed it. For example, a snowflake has a design that can be described as a six-fold radial symmetry, but nobody suggests it was designed that way. Its form developed because the six-fold crystalline structure of its original ice molecule attracted a condensation of water vapor that continues that pattern as it descends through the atmosphere. Because the snowflake descends through varying conditions of temperature and humidity the extent of the accretions may vary in random ways, so we could say that the form of the individual snowflake evolves as a response to local conditions. In the form of a snowflake we can observe a design without requiring that there be a Designer. In fractals, too, we can see near-infinite series of designs that evolve, not by any conscious design decision, but by repetitive applications of a mathematical formula.

Winding Paley's Watch

In his book Natural Theology[35], published in 1802, William Paley (1743–1805), an English clergyman, cites the world of nature as proof for the existence of god. In his famous watchmaker analogy he asserts that just as the existence of a watch assumes the existence of a watchmaker, the existence of the world must assume the existence of a Creator. He writes:

> "In crossing a heath, suppose I pitched my foot against a stone, and were asked how the stone came to be there; I might possibly answer, that, for anything I knew to the contrary, it had lain there forever . . . But suppose I had found a watch upon the ground, and it should be inquired how the watch happened to be in that place; I should hardly think of the answer I had before given, that for anything I knew, the watch

> might have always been there. .... There must have existed, at some time, and at some place or other, an artificer or artificers, who formed [the watch] for the purpose which we find it actually to answer; who comprehended its construction, and designed its use. ...
>
> Every indication of contrivance, every manifestation of design, which existed in the watch, exists in the works of nature; with the difference, on the side of nature, of being greater or more, and that in a degree which exceeds all computation. . . . Upon the whole, after all the struggles of a reluctant philosophy, the necessary resort is to a Deity. Design must have had a designer. That designer must have been a person. That person is God."

Paley argued that the complex structures of living things and the remarkable adaptations of plants and animals required an intelligent designer. He accepted that some species change and adapt to a changing environment, but insists that the possibility for these changed forms was also programmed into the original design.

> "In the ordinary derivation of plants and animals from one another, a particle . . . determines the organization of a future body. This particle, from which springs and by which is determined a whole future nature, itself proceeds from and owes its constitution to a prior body; nevertheless . . . the incepted organization, is not corrupted by a corruption, or destroyed by its dissolution; but, on the contrary, is sometimes extricated and developed by those very causes — survives and comes into action, when the purpose for which it was prepared comes into use. . . . In the most general case, that, as we have said, of the generation of plants and animals made from one another, the latent

organization is either similar to the old organization, or has the power of communicating to new matter the old organic form. But it is not restricted to this rule. There are other cases . . . in which [the organization} suits with a different situation to which it is destined."

He wrote this half-a-century before Charles Darwin published his 1859 book: On the Origin of Species[36]. In his Introduction Darwin wrote:

"As many more individuals of each species are born than can possibly survive; and as, consequently, there is a frequently recurring struggle for existence, it follows that any being, if it vary however slightly in any manner profitable to itself, under the complex and sometimes varying conditions of life, will have a better chance of surviving, and thus be *naturally selected*. From the strong principle of inheritance, any selected variety will tend to propagate its new and modified form."

This was condensed into an elegantly brief 10-word summary by Richard Dawkins[37]

"All life evolves by the differential survival of replicating entities".

It would have been such an interesting encounter if Paley and Darwin could have met. Darwin had discovered a world even more wonderful than that considered by Paley, a world that had the capability of creating itself. Paley's Natural Theology used nature as supporting evidence for his belief in god. By making the world more wonderful, Paley could have made his god more wonderful. In his final chapter of The Origin of Species Darwin wrote:

"There is grandeur in this view of life, with its several powers, having been originally breathed into a few forms or into one; and that, whilst this planet has gone cycling on according to the fixed law of gravity, from so simple a beginning endless forms most beautiful and most wonderful have been, and are being, evolved."

In comparison with this magnificent perspective the overview of creationists, those who reject evolution, are naïve, self-centered, and ugly. Jake Hebert of the Institute for Creation Research in Dallas asserts that many of the properties of our universe appear to have been engineered or "fine-tuned" in order to make our existence possible, the so-called Anthropic Coincidences. If the world had been a little bit hotter, or a little bit colder, or with a bit less oxygen, or a bit more water, or with more gravity or less sunlight, we would not have been able to survive. I think he has got it exactly wrong. I see no evidence that the universe has been "engineered" at all, much less that it has been "engineered" to suit us. Any process of "fine-tuning" has been applied to ourselves through selective evolution. Alternate versions of humankind that might have been able to survive on other worlds in atmospheres of ammonia did not survive on ours. Even the Book of Genesis did not make that error—the world was created several days before humanity (on that at least we can agree!) and Adam and Eve and all their friends and relations had to adapt to whatever conditions they found here. Creationists maintain that their god created a huge play-pen, just for us, and we get to rule the entire kindergarten. If we behave badly we might get spanked later, but meanwhile there is nothing to prevent us bringing-down the whole show. Paley did not reject evolution—the concept had not yet been formulated in his lifetime—but he did reject the closed-mind attitude of creationists, saying "The true theist will be the first to listen to *any* credible communication of divine knowledge. Nothing that has been learned through Natural Theology will diminish his desire for further instruction, or his disposition to receive it in humility and thankfulness."

Why Are We Here? 81

The watch against which William Paley stumbled on his walk across a heath, and which was celebrated by Richard Dawkins in the title of his 1996 book "The Blind Watchmaker"[38], was designed to tell the time. That was the purpose for which the watchmaker created it. His design, like all design, had a purpose.

What was he purpose of the stone which Paley kicked against? Could it be that it was created 140 million years ago so that at the end of the 18th Century it would trip up an Anglican clergyman out for a walk and cause him to look down and notice somebody had dropped a watch which would inspire him by comparing the two to create an analogy leading him to a popular but false conclusion that "every indication of contrivance, every manifestation of design, which existed in the watch, exists in the works of nature."? Was it the purpose of the designer of the world of nature to design a world of nature which would have the recursive purpose of demonstrating that the world of nature has a purpose, and that purpose is to demonstrate . . . in an infinite regress? Or could it be that the world has not (yet?) got a purpose? As children we used to sing a simple hymn[39]:

> "God is working His purpose out/
> as year succeeds to year.
> God is working His purpose out/
> and the time is drawing near."

which implies that even for people of faith the Universe is a work in progress. That means—it's evolving! and its purpose, if any, is also evolving. Right now, its purpose is to be itself.

NOTES for Chapter Five

[31] Courtesy of the Cleveland Museum of Art/The Wade Collection
[32] At a talk at Expo67 in Montreal
[33] George Bernard Shaw, Androcles and the Lion, 1912
[34] T.S. Eliot, Ash Wednesday, 1930, Faber & Faber Ltd.
[35] William Paley, Natural Theology, or Evidences of the Existence and Attributes of the Deity collected from the Appearances of Nature, London and Philadelphia, 1802.
[36] Charles Darwin, On the Origin of Species by Means of Natural Selection, or the Preservation of Favoured Races in the Struggle for Life, 1859. London: John Murray.
[37] Richard Dawkins, The Selfish Gene (1976) Oxford University Press
[38] Richard Dawkins, The Blind Watchmaker: Why the Evidence of Evolution Reveals a Universe without Design, 1996. W.W. Norton & Company, London, New York.
[39] No 548 in The English Hymnal, from a poem by Arthur Ainger (1894)

CHAPTER SIX

Cosmic FAQ No. 3 : Where are we going?

Again "where" implies there is a place, and "we" implies there is an "us" that can go there. If this question is more than a request for travel directions it is a leading question.

Life is defined as "The animate existence or the term of animate existence of an individual or animal."

Death is defined as "The end of life; the total and permanent cessation of all vital functions of an animal or plant."

Sometimes people who have been pronounced dead and show no vital signs recover. Sometimes these individuals report having seen bright lights, shining angels, and other heavenly images during these episodes. Their experiences have been quoted as evidence of an after-life of which these individuals have been given a sneak preview.

There is a much simpler explanation. First, by definition, a temporary absence of detectable vital signs does not indicate death. Absence of evidence is not evidence of absence.[40] So these individuals did not return from the dead; they never were dead because death is, by definition, permanent. Their temporary lack of vital signs just points to some limitations in our diagnostic capabilities.

Second, their visions of a Shining Path do not necessarily attest to a spiritual reality. Experiments with mice have shown that when the blood supply to the brain is restricted the visual cortex shows increased stimulation — mouse visions of a mouse-heaven, so the reports by comatose patients of their having seen a celestial light show could be accurate, but the vision could have been clinically induced. While these subjects were comatose and without heartbeat it could well be that a reduced blood flow could lead to effects in the brain that would later be remembered as shining lights, possibly to be interpreted as visions of eternity. It is always the memory of these visions that is reported, after the event, and not the visions themselves as works in progress.

Visions may also be induced by chemical stimulus. In 1953 Aldus Huxley experimented with mescalin, a psychotropic drug, which gave him mystical insights into the world around him. He pointed out[41] that the mystical visions of some of the saints could also have an explanation that was purely physical. They lived in remote times (and sometimes in inaccessible places) where medical care was less available. An abscessed tooth could filter all sorts of poisons into the bloodstream, and the ensuing intoxication could give rise to hallucinations which were reported as spiritual insights. Prolonged fasting, too, could cause the body to absorb toxins that would otherwise be excreted, giving rise to mystical transports. Perhaps that was the attraction of the anchorite's life: all the hardships were more than compensated for by visions that were interpreted as being divine.

Spiritualists, mediums and clairvoyants claim to have communication with the residual spirits of dead people, and thereby assert, like all religions, that there is some form of life that continues after physical death. The practitioner enters a trance state, invokes the presence of the spirit of a dead person who was formerly known to the querent, perhaps a relative, and passes on messages of hope and inspiration together with some items of personal information of which the practitioner could not possibly have had any knowledge.

This is held out as proof that there is communication with the dead, or rather, that the dead can communicate with us, and if that is so there must be an afterlife in which the dead are not all that dead. However, there is a more economical explanation. The information about the dead person is not known to the practitioner but it is known by the querent, so if the practitioner has some ability to read the querent's mind a few crumbs of that private information could become available. If it is accepted that all individuals exist as individuations of a universal consciousness some degree of cross-communication or telepathy could be present. This ability, plus skill in reading body language and emotional responses could provide enough items of background information to establish the appearance of a connection with the spirit world, even if such a world does not exist. This does not imply that all mediums are fraudulent, although some are. I am sure that some of them are not aware of the source of the information they are disclosing and interpret the communication as coming from the dearly departed, when in fact it is being communicated by the living person sitting opposite. The skill of a medium is judged by the ability to give the querent messages that are redundant, to impart to him information that is he already has—a recursive communication that implies that a former loved one is now enduring eternal life.

Sometimes eternal life is hard to avoid. When Fr. John Beach, a Chaplain at Trinity College, was celebrating Mass he would use the words "The Body of our Lord Jesus Christ given for you; preserve your body and soul unto everlasting life." To speed things up he would economize in the words of administration, giving one communicant the Body of Christ and the next one the Everlasting Life –we were supposed to share. Then I noticed that in his administration there was a polarity. In the line-up at the altar the odd-numbered communicants, numbers 1, 3, 5, 7 . . . would receive the Body of Christ while the even-numbered ones, numbers 2, 4, 6, 8 . . . would receive the Everlasting Life. I did not mind the Body of Christ but I found the concept of Eternal Life repulsive, so by positioning myself an odd number of places from the beginning of the line I could be assured of avoiding eternity. Sometimes I had to do a square dance doh-si-doh with number 9 so I could become number 9 in his place, displacing him to slot number 10, but alas it did not always work. One of the people on my right settled for a blessing instead, throwing the whole system out of whack, so I had to miss out on the Body of Christ and opt for a blessing too. Sometimes its hard to be a Christian and an Atheist both.

Great Heavens Above

For Cosmic FAQ No. 3, "Where Are We Going?" many answers have been provided, but with little agreement among them. Each religion appears to have its own real-estate holdings in a sort of Florida-in-the-sky where hundreds of gated retirement facilities abut one another. Many of these are seven-storey constructions where the prestigious penthouse is reserved for the elect. Here is a brief prospectus for a selection of these venues.

Catholic Heaven

The Catholic Heaven is most impressive of all the heavenly mansions. It is the seven-storey abode for angels, and for the souls of the just. According to Dante, beneath Heaven there are nine levels of basement and sub-basement. If the heavenly mansion is built above the sky these sub-celestial basements should penetrate down through the sky into the Universe where they should be visible from Earth with a sufficiently powerful telescope. Perhaps that is what black holes are—darkly attractive regions where gravitation is so strong that those who enter must abandon all hope of leaving. There are many many black holes, offering accommodation for Catholic sinners numbered in the billions: a rate of incarceration that exceeds even that of some of the more totalitarian earthly regimes.

Between these two constructions there is Purgatory, a place from which Catholic sinners can eventually be released into house-arrest, either by providing bail money funded by the prior purchase of indulgences while on earth, by the supplications of those surviving, or by opting for an imposition of community service. Besides accommodation for the general population Purgatory has two minimum-security wings, the Limbus Infantium and the Limbus Patrum. The first named is for the unbaptized who die in infancy, or for those too young to have committed personal sins but are still guilty of original sin, or for those too young to confess their sins and receive absolution. The children's hymn[42]

"There's a home for little children
Above the bright blue sky,
Where Jesus reigns in glory,
A home of peace and joy."

applies only to those good little Catholic children who had made their confessions and received absolution before being taken. The rest, if they are lucky, will be consigned to the Limbus Infantium, a sort of permanent day-care centre in the sky where they will be well looked-after but will never have a heavenly home.

The Limbus Patrum is a retirement home for those patriarchs and prophets who were of service to the church but could not enter Heaven immediately as they had never been baptized. This condition would be replaced by permanent bliss when the Messianic Kingdom is established, and Jesus personally would come down and baptize them and conduct them back into Heaven. The enrollment would include such celebrities as Moses, Abraham, Isaac, Jacob and David. Below the level of limbus there are eight levels of basement, each offering a punishment appropriate for those guilty of committing each of the seven deadly sins, which include lust, greed, anger, heresy, violence, envy and sloth.

Jehovah's Heaven

At the opposite extreme, the Heaven for Jehovah's Witnesses is the smallest facility; almost a boutique heaven. Occupancy is restricted to 144,000 souls, a population approximately equal to that of Fort Lauderdale. Here on Earth the Witnesses show great altruism in going door-to-door to promote this residence because very few of the Witnesses themselves would qualify for admission. As laid out in Revelations 14: 1–5, immigration is restricted to 144,000, and those selected must be male, virgins, and Jewish. It is possible that there are still some vacancies.

Anglican Heaven

Anglican Heaven is a spacious celestial landscape of manor houses and bishop's palaces, with servants quarters round the back, because this is the eternal abode of the aristocracy. Each manor house has its own village with its own village church which offers a living, an eternal one, to a poor priest. Between these estates there are woodlands where the shooting is excellent, replete with grouse, partridge, pheasant and pigeon, and every day the fox-hunt is the major social event of the Church's year, followed by the Hunt Ball.

There is no Anglican Hell. We just don't talk about such things. When he was still an Anglican John Henry Newman[43] wrote:

> "If we wished to imagine a punishment for an unholy, reprobate soul, we perhaps could not fancy a greater than to *summon it to heaven*. Heaven would be hell to an irreligious man. We know how unhappy we

are apt to feel at present, when alone in the midst of strangers, or of men of different tastes and habits from ourselves. How miserable, for example, would it be to have to live in a foreign land, among a people whose faces we never saw before, and whose language we could not learn. And this is but a faint illustration of the loneliness of a man of earthly dispositions and tastes, thrust into the society of saints and angels. How forlorn would he wander through the courts of heaven! He would find no one like himself; he would see in every direction the marks of God's holiness, and these would make him shudder."

I have to agree. For me, Hell would be a place full of happy smiling Christians: Calvin College in the Clouds. Isaac Asimov[44] agrees: "I don't believe in an afterlife, so I don't have to spend my whole life fearing hell, or fearing heaven even more. For whatever the tortures of hell, I think the boredom of heaven would be even worse."

Mark Twain recommended "Go to Heaven for the climate, Hell for the company", but George Bernard Shaw cautioned " Hell is full of musical amateurs." and Jean-Paul Sartre[45] agreed "Hell is other people."

Glorious Heaven

For the lower classes, those who are not members of the establishment and would not qualify for the Anglican heaven, The Salvation Army has sponsored a heaven which is that ultimate posting for those troopers who are Promoted to Glory. Here they can experience an eternity of brass bands with an accompaniment of handballs and tambourines. This spirit was captured by Vachel Lindsay (1879-1931), an American poet, in his 1913 poem "General William Booth Enters Heaven". Booth was the founder of The Salvation Army. Here is the first verse:

"Booth led boldly with his big bass drum—
(Are you washed in the Blood of the Lamb?)
The Saints smiled gravely, and they said, 'He's come.'
(Are you washed in the Blood of the Lamb?)
Walking lepers followed, rank on rank,
Lurching bravos from the ditches dank,
Drabs from the alleyways and drug fiends pale—
Minds still passion-ridden, soul-powers frail;
Vermin-eaten saints with moldy breath,
Unwashed legions with the ways of Death—
(Are you washed in the Blood of the Lamb?)"

The Salvation Army is noted for its work among the poor, the homeless and the addicted. It's focus is more on rescuing those who are experiencing a present Hell, rather than in promising a future Heaven.

Jewish Heaven

I don't know whether there is such a place; or if there is, I don't know whether there are any residents. God's dwelling place is mentioned in Psalm 68 v.5, but there is no mention that he is taking in house-guests. All the Jewish people I know are so burdened with guilt I can't imagine any of them enjoying an eternity of bliss. In a seminar led by Rabbi Steven Saltzman[46] he said:

> "There is no forgiveness in Judaism.
> "If you commit the crime you do the time.
> "Only g-d can forgive, and he doesn't!"

Some people seeking relief from such a burden have opted for alternate ultimate outcomes, such as a Catholic Heaven for Fr. Gregory Baum, and a Nirvana for Baba Ram Dass (né Richard Alpert).

Muslim Heaven

"For believers Allah has promised beautiful mansions of everlasting bliss set in Gardens of Eternity with rivers flowing beneath them. They will be adorned with bracelets of gold and will wear green garments of fine silk and heavy brocade. Cups of delicious wine from a clear-flowing fountain will be passed to them but they will not suffer any intoxication. Beside them will be chaste women restraining their glances with eyes big with wonder and beauty. The believers will recline on couches arranged in ranks with rich carpets spread out, where they will be joined to maidens with beautiful, big and lustrous eyes like well-guarded pearls, whom no man or Jinn has ever touched before them."[47]

I thought there wasn't much here that would appeal to a woman, most of the female residents appeared to be on staff, so I asked my friend Samirah how would she like to spend a lifetime of eternity. She replied "With a man who listens!".

A hadith, or religious tradition based on the words of the Prophet[48], states that a warrior who has given his life in a jihad or religious struggle becomes a Shahid, or martyr, and is guaranteed entry into heaven where he will be attended by seventy-two virgins. I can see how such a future could be attractive to teenage boys and might be a factor in encouraging them to enroll, but for me the prospect fills me with horror. I can imagine no fate more terrifying than to be forced to spend eternity with seventy-two 17-year-olds. They would gang up on me. They would be forever chattering about their ankle-chains, their lip-gloss, their movie magazines. The noise would be deafening, and it would go on and on and on. It would be enough to make me pray! "O save me! Anything but this! I shouldn't even be here! I'm an Anglican!"

Mansions for Heavenly Masons

For Freemasons the Great Lodge in the Sky created by GAOTU, the Great Architect of the Universe, is the opposite to Muslim Heaven—there are no women at all, and one needs a secret handshake to get in. The dress code is also different—there are no shining robes. Instead, white aprons with blue trim and gold dangles are worn over conservative business suits. There is a pipeline (up from Hell) that delivers forty different brands of scotch to the bar, and an exhaust fan that blows the cigar smoke back down again to the basement.

From his throne in the East the Worshipful Master rules and governs his Lodge, guiding the Brethren through their accomplishing of the everlasting Work, and seeing that every member shall have his due. On lesser thrones in the West and South the Senior and Junior Wardens preside. The Junior Warden presides over the lunch break, calling the Brethren from labor to refreshment, and from refreshment to labor. Refreshment consists of sandwiches where bread shining with all the whiteness of innocence enfolds pink circles of bologna, orange squares of Kraft cheese, and ellipses of green pickle.

In the centre, under the aegis of the Great Architect of the Universe, the Rough Ashlar is made Perfect, King Solomon's Temple is restored, and the Secrets that were lost are found again.

Pet Heaven

"Just this side of heaven is a place called Rainbow Bridge. When an animal dies that has been especially close to someone here, that pet goes to Rainbow Bridge.

"There are meadows and hills for all of our special friends so they can run and play together. There is plenty of food, water and sunshine, and our friends are warm and comfortable.

"All the animals who had been ill and old are restored to health and vigor; those who were hurt or maimed are made whole and strong again, just as we remember them in our dreams of days and times gone by. The animals are happy and content, except for one small thing; they each miss someone very special to them, who had to be left behind.

"They all run and play together, but the day comes when one suddenly stops and looks into the distance. His bright eyes are intent; his eager body quivers. Suddenly he begins to run from the group, flying over the green grass, his legs carrying him faster and faster. You have been spotted, and when you and your special friend finally meet, you cling together in joyous reunion, never to be parted again. The happy kisses rain upon your face; your hands again caress the beloved head, and you look once more into the trusting eyes of your pet, so long gone from your life but never absent from your heart. Then you cross Rainbow Bridge together..." (Author unknown)

Even St. Francis of Assisi, who numbered the animal kingdom among his brothers and sisters, would not stretch his theology so far. However the concept gave great comfort to my friend Eleanor who fully expected to cross Rainbow Bridge some fine day where she would be reunited with Tara, Ripper, Bucky, Taker, Gainer, Catcher, Oriel, Chimney, Iggy (Ignatius), Barkley and Digby.

Ultimate Choice

It could be thought that such a great range of available Heavens would provide consumers with many options, but as a practical matter this is not the case. Each Heaven is offered as part of a unique package deal that includes transportation, and no substitutions are allowed. If one wished to change destinations one would have to change carriers and lose ones deposit, so people tend to stay with their original choice, if in fact they had any choice at all. Happy Holidays!

NOTES for Chapter Six

[40] Martin Rees, quoted in The Yale Book of Quotations, ed. Fred R. Shapiro, Yale University Press. 2006.
[41] Aldus Huxley, The Doors of Perception, 1954, Chatto and Windus.
[42] No 500 in Hymns for the Church Catholic, No 607 in The English Hymnal, based on a poem by Albert Midlane (1859)
[43] John Henry Newman, Holiness Necessary for Future Blessedness. Parochial Sermons, 1834.
[44] Isaac Asimov, from "On Religiosity" in Free Inquiry magazine (Jan 1992)
[45] "L'enfer, c'est les autres" from the J-P Sartre play "No Exit". 1944, Vintage International.
[46] Steven Saltzman, in a Liturgy Seminar at the Toronto School of Theology, November 20, 2014
[47] The Holy Qur'an, suras 9:72, 18:31, 37:45, and 52:20
[48] Al-Hayat Al-Jadida Palestinian Authority Daily, Jan. 2 2004.

CHAPTER SEVEN

Heavenly Warfare

Millions have been slaughtered in the name of religion. Some writers have been adding them up and comparing the total with the number of deaths from other disasters to prove a point, but I am not going to do that. One such death is too many.

There are four motivations for this religious violence:
- personal conversion,
- credal dominance,
- political consolidation, and
- territorial gain.

In the scriptures of various faiths there is little, if any, support for violence or coercion in attempting to induce a person to accept a different religious belief. The Qur'an has many admonitions advocating fierce behavior in dealing with the Unbeliever, but these are all related to pitched battles between opposing armies or dealing with a person who has renounced Islam. There are just two references[49] dealing with individuals who have a different religion, and they both say: don't get involved, agree to differ . . .

> "I will not worship that which you have been wont to worship, nor will you worship that which I worship.
> To you then be your way, and to me mine" (109:4)

. . . and Allah will take care of the situation later.

> "So make no haste against them [Unbelievers] for We but count out to them a (limited) number (of days)."

Muslims have quoted these texts to illustrate the essentially peaceable nature of Islam, but the situation is not quite so straightforward. There are many commentaries, or hadiths, that support violence or the punishments of sharia law, and with some people these have acquired canonical status, although the Sunni and Shia factions accept different compilations. In practical terms these are just as influential as the Qur'an itself. The situation is similar to developments in the church, where later doctrines such as The Holy Trinity were overlaid upon biblical scripture.

In dealing with the unbeliever Jesus too advocated nothing more violent than shaking the dust off one's feet[50] if one's message was not accepted. This I interpret not as a hostile act but as a way of "letting-go" of a disappointment in order to be free to move on to the next encounter. In the 19th century this gentle approach was adopted by David Willson, the leader of The Children of Light, a break-away Quaker sect in southern Ontario. Willson wrote[51]

> "We are not perfect, but the system adopted by us is justified of God in scripture, and draws the soul near unto God in Christ. We use no persuasions to others to believe in our theory, knowing all things are the Lord's, and he disposes of them according to his own mind; and that the human heart hath no right to move in the things of God."

Others did not have such scruples, and did not shrink from effecting conversion by coercion. This would include the Catholic Inquisition in Spain and Portugal, Calvin's tribunals in Geneva, Cromwell's essays into Ireland, the Crusades in Jerusalem, the Shi'ite Assassins in the Arab world who gave their name to such perpetrators, and the slaughter of Canaanites, Midianites, Moabites, and Ephraimites in Biblical times. To quote Mark Twain again: "[Man] has made a graveyard of the globe in trying his honest best to smooth his brother's path to happiness and heaven."

Why the violence? Because *all* religious beliefs defy logic, so argument cannot be used to establish the absolute right-ness of any one of them. Extermination is the only way forward. What made these Holy Wars so holy was the fact that God fought on both sides. The motto "Gott mit Uns" (God with Us) was embossed on belt buckles of the German army, the same sentiment is expressed on the American dollar bill. The popular song "Praise the Lord, and pass the ammunition" refers to an incident in the Second World War when the U.S.S. New Orleans at anchor in Pearl Harbor was attacked by the air force of the Heavenly Emperor of Japan. The Chaplain (aka the Sky Pilot) demonstrated a fusion of both his military and religious roles by putting down his Bible to join the battle:

"Up jumped the sky pilot, gave the boys a look
And manned the gun himself
as he laid aside The Book, shouting
'Praise the Lord and pass the ammunition!
Praise the Lord, we're on a mighty mission!
Praise the Lord and pass the ammunition!
And we'll all stay free!'"

In Jerusalem the orthodox Hassidim may show their disapproval of cars being driven on the sabbath by throwing stones at them, thus violating the sabbath to protest sabbath violations. Anger trumps obligation.

The motivations for most of the world's Holy Wars have been to achieve an increase in political influence, economic dominance, or territorial expansion. The religious rationale was just a gloss of sanctity that military leaders laid over their operations to encourage their troops to fight more fiercely. Somehow their theology could be adjusted to circumscribe Jesus' words[52] to "love your enemies" and "turn the other cheek". Those doctrines are suitable only for times of peace. Times of peace are great, but sometimes peace is under attack and we need a Just War to rescue it. All governments have Departments of Defence whose role is to preserve peace by having the greatest possible capability of attacking others. This readiness to sacrifice others was celebrated by The Fugs in Tuli Kupferberg's lyrics "Kill, kill, kill for peace!".

Holy wars are an extreme of evangelism but they have had no great record of success as a means of promoting one's faith by converting others to adopt one's theology. A much more efficient way to advance the market share of one's theology is simply to kill off all the competition. Sometimes in the heat of battle it is difficult to determine the faith of the combatants. Pope Innocent III had a solution to this problem. When his troops asked how could they tell which of their Christian captives were the Albigensian enemy he commanded them "Kill them all. God will know His own!".

Some combatants who consider themselves involved in a holy war may be called terrorists. This is a self-referencing declaration which is self-fulfilling because one becomes a terrorist by being declared to be one. This declaration creates a permanent truth, an article of faith which does not need to be supported by any external evidence. The term is reserved for those whom one does not like. If we approve of the efforts of a group practising terrorism they become Freedom Fighters. The four essential ingredients that need to be present for terrorism to flourish are:

>A democratic regime,
>A repressed minority,
>A religious distinction between factions, and
>A difference in culture or language.

Terrorism can flourish only in a democracy, where there is the possibility of influencing a regime change. All our recent high-minded attempts to displace dictatorships with democracies have created terrorism where none existed before. In a dictatorship such a movement would be stamped-out in short order. This has caused some embarrassment in the West. George W. Bush was a principled supporter of democracy as long as it continued to elect him, but he had some problems when faced with the reality of the democritically elected Hamas in Gaza, and the democratically elected Muslim Brotherhood in Egypt, neither of which he liked. The Muslim Brotherhood had been deprived of its political power by the President of Egypt, Hosni Mubarak. It morphed into a social regime, providing health clinics, sports clubs, schools, and community facilities, and was well-regarded by the public, just like the Salvation Army. When the Mubarak regime was overthrown the Muslim Brotherhood reverted to its former political role with the intention of creating an Islamic state, until it was dissolved by an Army coup which labelled it as a terrorist organization. Is the Salvation Army just waiting for a similar opportunity to deploy its forces to achieve world domination? Could it too be proclaimed a terrorist organization? The Salvation Army already has a military-style chain-of-command in place. Their publication is The War Cry, and their motto "Blood and Fire!". Their battle hymn "Onward Christian Soldiers" with its thundering tonic-and-dominant bass instills fear into the hearts of the atheists as these Soldiers of Christ arise and put their armor on.

> "Onward Christian Soldiers
> Marching as to war pom-pom-pom
> With the Cross of Jesus
> Going on before."

Atheists have no history of instigating a holy war to persuade others to accept their beliefs. Would they be vulnerable to an attack by the armed might of the Salvation Army? Should we be afraid?

Atheist Anger Management

It is strange that atheists should be regarded as angry, argumentative people. Most atheists do not wish to engage in debates with people of faith. They see no common ground where gaps between their positions could be bridged, so with few exceptions they refuse to engage in debates. Atheists accept Pascal's epigram

"The heart has its reasons which reason knows nothing of:

We know the truth not only by the reason, but by the heart."

but they realise that "the reason" and "the heart" generate different truths. John Keats (1795-1821) in the final couplet of Ode to a Greek Urn:

"Beauty is truth, truth beauty, — that is all

Ye know on earth, and all ye need to know."

revealed that our recognition of truth is by our appreciation of its beauty, whether this is the inspiration of a religious truth or the mathematical elegance of a scientific deduction. At the time of their inception (or conception?) most religious doctrines were compatible with the state of advancement of scientific knowledge of their time. Generally, there was no conflict between the permanent religious truth and the provisional scientific observations that happened to be accepted at that time. But times change, and the provisional truths changed with them while the permanent truths did not. The gap between the truths became more extreme, and as the gap widened the energy required to bridge the gap increased. Originally most of the tenets of a permanent truth were seen as a reasonable explanation of the cosmos and the human society within it. Exceptions to the natural order that were presented as miracles and healings were cited as examples of the superiority of the permanent truth over the provisional truth. This argument was an "own goal", where a team accidentally kicks a ball into its own net. People of faith may declaim that God's will is superior to the Laws of Science, and miracles and healings are evidence for the existence of God, but scientists will dispute that premise, saying the researcher in the next lab will also be superior to the Laws of Science if his experiment to disprove one of those "Laws" is successful. Does that make him a god?

To continue to assert the superiority of the permanent truth over the more advanced versions of the accepted provisional truth required an opposite transition in believers. Many believers who were reasonable people originally had to develop into fanatics if they wished to maintain their beliefs in the face of all evidence to the contrary. As science advanced the logic of those continuing to adhere to a permanent truth became more strained as contrary evidence piled up. Science was evolving at an exponentially increasing rate, and changes that had previously taken centuries to evolve were now being accomplished in a few years. Every day there is news of some new scientific breakthrough, and the custodians of these breakthroughs are, in the main, atheists. We are seeing therefore, at the same time, an increase in atheism and an increase in religious fanaticism. Eric Hoffer[53] observes "The opposite of the religious fanatic is not the fanatical atheist but the gentle cynic who cares not whether there is a god or not."

Atheists have often been presented as not-very-nice people, cold and unfeeling, embittered and untrustworthy, and hostile to true believers whom they attack at every opportunity, even religious leaders. How rude! There may be some truth in this assertion, but not very much. The assertion does not need much of a foundation of truth because this is another permanent truth which endures despite evidence to the contrary. The only occasions I have seen where atheists have been argumentative is when religious people attempt to curtail the freedoms of atheists by imposing their will on them, or anybody else. This was the situation in the Montreal suburb of Dorval where a group of Muslim parents attempted to ban pork from the canteens of all the public schools. For health reasons banning pork might not be a bad thing, but a ban should not be imposed on the rest of us to ensure conformity with the dietary law of a particular religion.

If one's religion, what one believes, is just a choice, why is belief in a permanent truth so passionate? How can it motivate believers to propagate their faith even to the extent of killing-off those who do not believe? If it's just a choice how can it inspire such disdain for others, such hatred of other beliefs? The answer is: it's just a choice, but it's *our* choice. We identify with it, and we allow it to identify us. Some of us become so identified with our religions that when atheists reject all religion we feel that they are rejecting us as people. We allow our religion to distinguish us, and such a distinction may separate us from the rest of humankind who thereby cease to be our brothers and sisters. There is an element of hostility in the term "Unbeliever" because that implies that belief in some sort of a supreme being is the standard from which atheists have fallen short. Belief is a concept added to humanity, not a concept that has been subtracted from atheists. According to Carl Sagan "Atheism is an attitude, a frame of mind that looks at the world objectively, fearlessly, always trying to understand all things as a part of nature." According to Richard Dawkins[54] "We are all atheists about most of the gods that societies have ever believed in. Some of us just go one god further."

NOTES for Chapter Seven

[49] The Holy Qu'ran, 109:4 and 19:84, tr. Abdullah Yusuf Ali, 2003
[50] Mark 6:11.
[51] David Willson, A Short Word to Visitors to the Sharon Temple, 1831. see Emily McArthur, Children of Peace, 1898. York Pioneer and Historical Society.
[52] Matthew 5:44, Luke 6:29.
[53] Eric Hoffer, The True Believer, 2002.. Harper Modern Classics.
[54] Richard Dawkins "The Root of All Evil", UK Channel 4, 2006

CHAPTER EIGHT
Forging the Divinity of Jesus

To quote Mark Twain "If Christ were here now there is one thing he would not be—a Christian." Jesus never claimed to be God—nowhere in the gospels does he make that claim. But St. Paul, as a marketing executive, needed to promote Jesus to a divine status in order to sell Christianity to the Greeks. The Greek and Roman religions were headed up by gods, so Christianity needed a godhead too if it was going to compete. It was a case of keeping up with the Joves. Those striving to assert the divinity of Jesus put much stock in a couple of quotes from the gospel of John, 10:38 and 14:6

" . . . the Father is in me, and I in the Father." and

"No one comes to the Father except through me."

The gospel of John, the last of the canonical gospels, was probably written around the end of the first century, some sixty years after Jesus death, so it cannot be an eye-witness report, and the quotations attributed to Jesus do not sound like Jesus. They do not have the same pithy aphorisms that pepper his words in the other earlier gospels. They are exclusive and preachy. They sound more like some of the learned academic pronouncements I hear in the place of higher learning that employs me. It is even possible that the writer of the gospel of John (we don't know who he was) was influenced by some of the writings of Paul.

In the gospels there is little scriptural support for Jesus being god. Jesus makes many references to his Heavenly Father, but he does not claim that relationship to be an exclusive one. He shares a Heavenly Father with the rest of humanity. He mentions this on four occasions, when he is preaching...

"If you forgive men when they sin against you, your heavenly Father will also forgive you." Matthew 6:14.

"Look at the birds of the air, they do not sow or reap or store away in barns, and yet your heavenly Father feeds them." Matthew 6:26.

"So do not worry, saying 'What shall we eat?' or 'What shall we drink?' or 'What shall we wear?' for . . . your heavenly Father knows that you need them." Matthew 6:32.

"If you then, though you are evil, know how to give good gifts to your children, how much more will your Father in heaven give the holy spirit to those who ask him." Luke 11:13.

In each of these four instances where Jesus mentions "your heavenly Father" he indicates to his listeners that we all share a heavenly Father; but the most convincing support for that concept lies in Matthew 6:9 and Luke 11:2 where, in the opening phrase of the Lord's Prayer, he invites us to pray to Our Father, a filial relationship shared by all Christians.

Paul had problems with this. He felt that if Christianity was to compete with other religions where their leaders were gods, Jesus too had to be elevated to that status. He could not remain just a divinely inspired man. Now Paul never met Jesus, except during a hallucination on the road to Damascus, so he never cast eyes on him. It would have been interesting if he had. The only description we have of Jesus' appearance is in the writings of Flavius Josephus[55], a contemporary historian, Jewish, who was born in Jerusalem but became a Roman citizen. Writing in Greek, he described Jesus as . . .

" . . . a man of simple appearance, mature age, dark skin, small stature, three cubits high [about 4 feet 8 inches], hunchbacked, with a long face, long nose, and meeting eyebrows, so that they who see him might be affrighted, with scanty hair [but] with a parting in the middle of his head, after the manner of the Nazirites, and with an undeveloped beard."

Christian censorship removed this unflattering description from all the existing copies of Josephus' work "The Capture of Jerusalem"; except that they missed one copy, the Josephus Slavonicus manuscript which was recently discovered in the library of a monastery in Russia. What it presents is a far cry from the standard pictures of Gentle Jesus with kind eyes, a softly-permed hair-do and a neatly-trimmed beard, such as the one that my parents hung in my bedroom in the hope that something would rub off on me. A far cry from the ancient Greek's depictions of their gods, all of whom had the bodily beauty of Greek Gods. There is some controversy over whether the Slavonicus document is genuine. I am inclined to give it the nod because I can see no reason why anyone would want to forge it if it were false, and overwhelming reasons for suppressing it if it were genuine. If Jesus were in fact a hunchback that would explain his rapid expiry on the cross. There is some textural support for the validity of this description. In Luke 19:3 there is a story of Zacchæus, a chief tax collector, who joined the crowds to see Jesus but could not "because he was small of stature" so he climbed a sycamore tree to get a good view. This text leaves it unclear whether it is Jesus or Zacchæus that is small of stature. There is a 50 per cent chance that the reference is to Zacchæus, which is probably the reason why this account was not deleted in a subsequent makeover of the Gospels.

Also in "The Acts of John"[56], an apocryphal second century text that was not admitted into the New Testament canon, the writer sees Jesus and says

> "I was afraid and cried out, and he, turning about, appeared as a man of small stature, and caught hold

on my beard and pulled it and said to me: John, be not faithless but believing, and not curious."

Jesus needed a makeover before he could be introduced to the Greeks as a potential god. However, I must say I prefer the rough-and-ready character of the former Jesus with his pithy sayings, his inclusive humanity, his sense of humor (after all, he appointed the bumbling St. Peter to take over the leadership of his church) his humility and humanity, his determination and wisdom ... I prefer all that to the suave and aloof persona presented to us by John's gospel.

Promoting Jesus

Throughout history a virgin birth has been a requirement for those wishing to be recognized as gods; commencing with Horus whose mother Isis conceived him by artificial insemination on the banks of the Nile. Following that we have:

Krishna, born of the virgin Devaki, c. 1,200 BC.
Zoroaster, born of the virgin Dughdova, c. 1,100 BC.
Mithras, born of a virgin c. 600 BC.
Buddha, born of the virgin Maya c. 600 BC.
Balder, a Scandinavian god, born of the virgin Frigga
Quetzalcoatl, born of the virgin Chimalman after she swallowed an emerald.

All these virgin births were recorded in retrospect, long after the progeny had achieved celebrity status. Of Jesus it could almost be said he had two virgin births as the accounts in the gospels of Luke and Matthew are so different[57]. In Luke Jesus has a bucolic birth where he is placed in a manger and worshiped by shepherds. In Matthew he receives a state visit from a visiting delegation of astronomers from the East who are politically well-connected and are bearing valuable gifts.

However for Pope Pius X the real proof of Jesus' divinity was his ability to perform miracles. He demanded that Christians "accept and acknowledge" that miracles are the surest signs of the divinity of Christ. This is a strangely recursive argument. He demanded that Christians *believe* that miracles are the logical evidence of the physical foundation for what he demanded they believe. My head is spinning.

There are 37 miracles assigned to Jesus, of which 25 are healings. This is an impressive number, but comes nowhere near the number of healings on the television shows of Oral Roberts or Benny Hinn. Do we have to confer divine status on these gentlemen too?

With the discovery of the Dead Sea Scrolls some evidence has appeared that Jesus was part of the Essene community[58], a contemplative order that abandoned the sectarian rivalries of the Pharisees and the Sadducees and from 200 BC to 100 CE established a settlement in Qumran which they called "the Wilderness" in contrast to the corruption they found in the cities. Those remaining in Jerusalem they called "the dead", while they were "the living". Anybody leaving the order would become one of the dead, but on returning would be restored to life. If Lazarus had left the order and Jesus persuaded him to return this could be interpreted as "restoring the dead to life".

The Essenes had an initiation ceremony involving immersion, a forerunner of baptism. A candidate, after he had completed two years of study could be admitted to full membership, entitling him to drink wine[59]. This process was called "turning water into wine". Thus it is possible that the reports of two miracles in the Gospel of John; "The Raising of Lazarus" and "The Wedding in Cana"[60] could be literal interpretations of poetic descriptions, giving rise to reports of miraculous happenings that would be evidence of divine intervention, if they had happened.

The only miracle to be reported in all four gospels is "The Feeding of the 5,000". A crowd gathered on a hillside to hear Jesus preach. Five thousand of them were men. There were also women and children,[61] but these we did not bother to count. Predictably, none of the men brought food, except for a boy who had a snack of bread and fish. But the women had brought picnic baskets. We did not count the baskets, but at the end of the day twelve were used to gather up the trash[62]. It's hard to imagine that the women, especially those with children, would have come on a picnic without bringing some food, so a role I see for Jesus in this would be for him to invite everybody who had brought food to share it with everyone else as if this gathering were a forerunner of Woodstock, and that is probably the way it happened. I see this version as being much more in tune with Jesus' pastoral nature, an opportunity for people to learn sharing and caring and building a community, rather than just another episode of magic.

If this "miracle" were perceived as a magic trick or as an invocation of supernatural power the people would have learned nothing from it; but if it was seen as a response to Jesus' invitation to share our resources with our neighbors everybody would have had an experience of the Kingdom.

These miracles were all recorded well after the events they depicted: the most recent example was "Walking on the Water" which achieved miracle status in the 17th Century. Launcelot Andrewes, Bishop of Rochester, was supervising the English translation of the scriptures which in 1611 became the King James' Bible. One of the translators pointed out to him that the Greek text was ambiguous. The preposition "επι" (epsilon-pi-iota, sounds like a fraternity) which means "on", and occurs in the phrase "walking on the water", can also mean walking near or around the water. Which meaning should he give it? After some consideration Andrewes opted for another miracle, rather than a mere description of location, and so it came about.

–The remaining miracles are fishing stories, and like all fishing stories they became more miraculous with each telling. But is it obligatory for a god to demonstrate his godliness by performing miracles? In some ways I feel the miracles form a barrier between Jesus and the rest of humankind—by portraying Jesus as behaving more like a god he becomes less human—and these alleged miracles could be a distraction from some of Jesus' truly wonderful accomplishments which I will list in the next chapter. And what about the resurrection that so many people make such a fuss over? Really it's hardly worth bothering about—it was just a six-week stopover on a vertical travel plan.

Divine Multiplication

Paul had a problem. He had to create a new god, Jesus, without displacing or compromising the god whom Jesus described as his (and our) "Heavenly Father". He achieved this by proposing Jesus as "the Son of God" who would also be divine. However, giving words their normal meanings, the Son would always be secondary to the Father, so to give the Son equal standing he was proclaimed to be co-eternal with the Father and not created by the Father which would have implied that there was a time when the Father was God alone. There was still the problem that these two personages could imply a contrast, if not a conflict. To defuse any possible misunderstanding, two centuries later, Tertullian proposed adding a third member, the Holy Spirit, to the entourage. After a lot of debate this was codified by the Council of Nicea in 325 CE, who had the backing of the Emperor Constantine to enforce it. Thus the Holy Trinity was set up as a means of preserving the divinity that had been imposed on Jesus. At the same time it made any sort of union with Judaism or Islam difficult because those religions were founded on the basis of the singularity of god and they traditionally profess a concept of monotheism with a singular person as God. Islam considers Jesus a prophet but not divine. The Qur'an states[63] "In the name of Allah, Most Gracious, Most Merciful. Say He is Allah, the One and Only; Allah, the Eternal, Absolute; He begets not, nor is He begotten; and there is none like unto Him."

Triangulating the Square

In the process of religious conversion, when one chooses to accept a conjecture as absolute truth, there is no requirement for such a belief to be believable. One may be led to adopting beliefs that are fanciful, irrational, illogical, unsustainable or just plain daft. Wallace Stevens, an American poet, illustrated this[64] in his 1922 poem "The Emperor of Ice-Cream". His couplet:

"Let be be finale of seem.

The only emperor is the emperor of ice-cream."

illustrates this with the great economy that is available to the poet. In the first line he makes a choice: he accepts a permanent status for a provisional truth. In the second line, which echoes the exclusivity of the Mohammed's proclamation "There is no God but God" he indicates how it is possible to pledge total and exclusive allegiance to a non-existent entity. He demonstrates how one can defer to a totally imaginary personage, even one whose absolute authority derives not from a lectionary but from confectionary. In the beginning was vanilla . . .

Then the classic white of vanilla ice-cream was joined by the romantic pink of strawberry ice-cream. Strawberry ice-cream was not made of vanilla ice-cream, its genesis was that strawberry ice-cream "proceeded from" vanilla ice-cream. (Some theologians can already see where I am going with this.) In the world of ice-cream vanilla and strawberry co-existed in sweet harmony. I have an early-childhood memory of those days when ice-cream was either strawberry or vanilla. It would be served either in an edible cone or in a metal chalice from which it could be spooned out with a wooden spatula which added a taste of wood to the dessert.

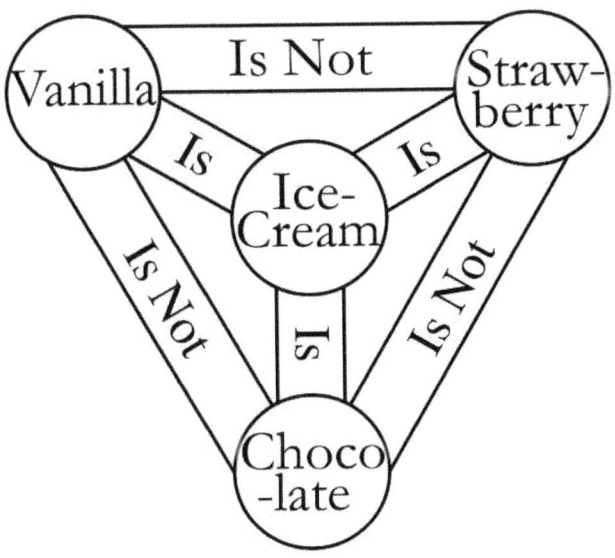

Fig. 10. The Scutum Fidei Shield of the Emperor of Ice-Cream

Then it was glorified! In the Lyons Corner House chain of restaurants strawberry and vanilla ice cream were served together in a confection known as Knickerbocker Glory. They were served in a tall glass with the addition of fruit syrup, chocolate sauce, whipped cream and a cherry on top. This required special cutlery—he who sups from a tall glass needs a long spoon. It was a special treat.

Later a third flavor was created—chocolate! This triune relationship was celebrated in the armorial bearings of the Emperor of Ice-Cream. His shield is illustrated in Fig. 10, and his imperial flag is a tricolor in pink-white-and-beige. The Shield, the Scutum Fidei, explains that vanilla, strawberry, and chocolate are wholly distinct flavors and yet each is wholly ice-cream. This mystical diagram was appropriated (without acknowledgement) by Christian theologians, who used it to explain the structure of the Trinity.

Now here's the question: Did chocolate ice-cream proceed from vanilla just like strawberry had done? Or did the existence of strawberry ice-cream open up the possibility for multiple flavors of ice-cream, so it could be said that chocolate ice-cream proceeded from both vanilla and strawberry? I've set up a flow chart to illustrate these two scenarios.

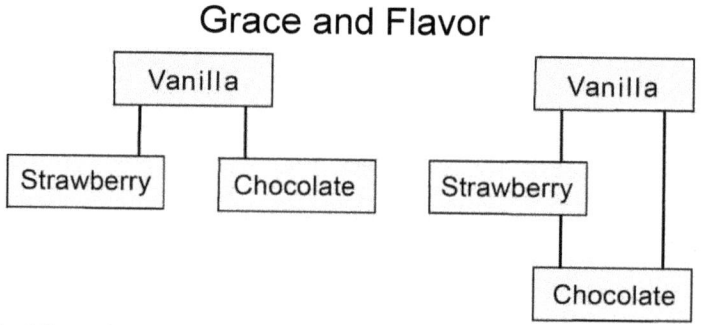

Fig.11. Alternate processes for development of chocolate ice-cream

Besides these two questions another more basic question comes to mind: Why would anyone care? I can't imagine even the most avid gelato-holic giving any time to such a debate; and yet a debate such as this has engaged and divided the Christian world for hundreds of years as the Filioque Controversy. "Filioque" is Latin for "and [from] the son".

The issue is how the church should set about setting-up the Holy Trinity. Substituting deities for desserts: did the Holy Spirit proceed from God-the-Father, as in the left-hand diagram, or did it proceed from God-the-Father and God-the-Son both, as in the right-hand diagram? The subject of this debate has much less substance than chocolate ice-cream which has a real presence—we can taste and see that the ice-cream is good—yet people got very upset about which version of the process should be believed. For atheists this preoccupation has to be The Divine Comedy, or perhaps Much Ado About Nothing; but for those that took it seriously

Fig. 12. Sundae services at the Church of God on Toronto's St. Clair Avenue.

it was very serious indeed. It marked a division between the Roman and Eastern Orthodox communions. For centuries Greek thought had been influenced by Plato[65], who proposed a dualism of mind-and-body, or matter-and-spirit. This dualism is found in the left-hand diagram, from which it can be deduced that both Son and Spirit proceed from the Father. This construct would be comfortable for the Greeks because it applies to the deities the duality of Son and Spirit, both proceeding from the Father. It can even be seen as being supported by Greek philosophy, cheers for the Home Team.

The Roman church preferred the right-hand diagram as this showed both the Father and the Son as having a role in the development of the Spirit. This additional role for the Son in the Holy Trinity enhanced the provenance of the Roman church because the church claimed St. Peter as its leader in a posthumous promotion, and he had been given that role by Jesus.

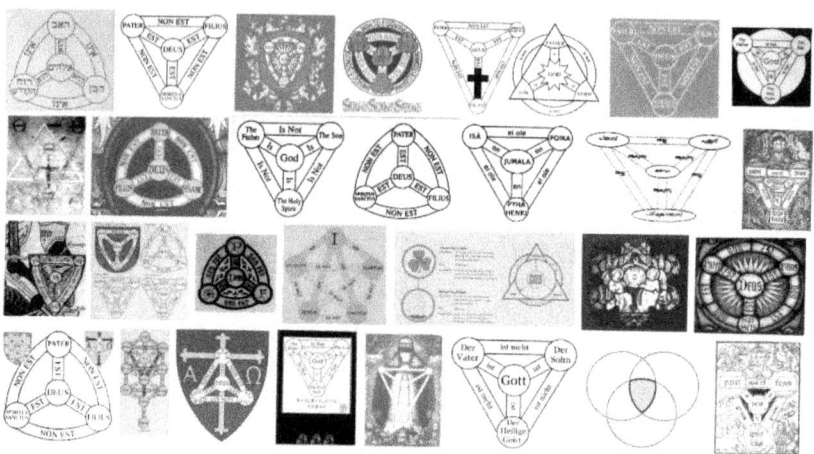

Fig. 13. Multiple expressions of the Scutum Fidei

Another problem with the triangular trinity is that chocolate is just the thin end of the wedge. If we can extend flavors to include chocolate, why stop there? We can diversify to include Butterscotch Ripple, Rocky Road and Crème de Menthe, embracing all the 31 flavors of Baskin Robbins. We can extend the range of the trinity to encompass the Greek panoply of deities, and all the 330 million Hindu gods. But the real argument against the Holy Trinity is that it is ugly. Saying that 3 = 1 tramps roughshod over the fundamental beauty of the sequence of natural numbers. It's not even accurate. If the combination of the Three Persons of the Trinity is also God, then my arithmetic adds up the members of the group to four, just as we can count the four circles in the form of the Scutum Fidei seen in Fig.10. The grouping may be expressed as: G_1, G_2, G_3 and G_{1+2+3}

The statement "Three in One and One in Three" is meaningless because it confuses the number of members in a group with the number of groups. It can have no meaning in number theory as a set cannot be a sub-set of itself.[66] If "One" is going to be "in Three" it must be cut up into thirds like three people sharing a pizza, otherwise it could never have been a "One" in the first place. The Scutum Fidei diagram is intentionally confusing, an attempt to project an aura of mystical significance by being purposefully irrational. There are hundreds of examples of this diagram—some are illustrated in Fig. 13. The most mystical, like the one at the centre of the bottom row, are those which are presided over by a being who has three semi-superimposed faces which share four eyes—you can't get more mystical than that. I have attempted to bring the diagram down to earth by applying it to something as mundane as ice-cream. This shows up a basic flaw: the diagram uses the same graphic to illustrate a relationship ("Is") and the absence of a relationship ("Is Not"). I cannot think of any other organization chart that uses a link to proclaim "This is not a link!".

The concept that all this obfuscation is attempting to mask is "Four".

Imagining God

Among the vast panoply of gods who are supervising the world is there room for one more? Imagine you are God; not any old god but that unknowable, ineffable, non-existent being that exists beyond knowing, and is as inscrutable as T.S. Eliot's cat. You are surrounded by statues, pictures, poems, images, manifestos and magicians put together by people claiming that these are you. Some of them are the work of visionaries, some were created by the majority vote of committees (whose resolutions became unanimous by extermination of the minority), and some were created for the prestige and profits they would generate. All these creations were created by people who set about creating uncreated gods. And while these gods are all different, the creators of each one are claiming that their particular creation is you. How do you feel about that? Some of them have created offspring for you, a son so you will have a closer connection with their humanity, and a holy ghost which would certainly be needed to come in and clean up when two bachelors are sharing an apartment. Some have turned you into a senior citizen, male of course, but without retirement benefits. Some have cast you in the forms of various animals—divine taxidermy. And some reduce you to a mere lump of metal or stone.

If I were you (and you were God) I would resent not so much the various images of Me that humans have created, but the arrogance with which they demand that I comply with their constructs, and the aggression with which they trash the constructs of others. In their sanctimonious holier-than-thou attitudes they are claiming to be holier than Me.

Among all these groups that are at one another's throats there is only one group that does not demand that I comply with their demands. There is only one group that does not attempt to fit me into their form. These are the atheists. They alone appreciate the beauty and wonder of my non-existence. Of all the faiths, sects, schisms and denominations this is the group that would be closest to my heart, if I had one.

NOTES for Chapter Eight

[55] Robert Eisler, The Messiah Jesus and John the Baptist according to Flavius Josephus' recently rediscovered 'Capture of Jerusalem' and other Jewish and Christian sources, 1931
[56] The Acts of John, ch 90, The Apocryphal New Testament, tr. M.R. James, 1924. Oxford: Clarendon Press.
[57] Luke 2: 6–20, Matthew 2: 9–12
[58] Christopher Knight & Robert Lomas, The Hiram Key, 1996. Century Books, Random House UK.
[59] Flavius Josephus, The Wars of the Jews, book 2.
[60] John 2: 1–11 and John 11: 1–45.
[61] Matthew 14: 21
[62] Matthew 14: 20
[63] The Holy Qur'an, sura 112, Purity of Faith
[64] Wallace Stevens, Collected Poems, 1954. Alfred A. Knopf Inc.
[65] Plato: Phaedo, ed. C.J.Rowe. 1993, Cambridge University Press.
[66] G. Spencer Brown, Laws of Form. 1996, George Allen and Unwin.

CHAPTER NINE

Following the Secular Jesus

If we were to take away from Jesus:
  his annunciation and virgin birth
  being the only son of God
  his living without sin
  all the miracles
  the resurrection
  his descending into Hell
  rising on the third day
  the ascension into Heaven, and
  his becoming the Judge of the living and the dead –
what's left? The answer is "Everything!" When Jesus is freed from all this doctrinal clutter he is still the greatest teacher the world has ever known.

As a leader: he laid the foundations for a community that would be supportive, sustaining and satisfying: a just society.

As a priest: his message was of courage, tolerance, peace and love.

Jesus as Teacher

Jesus' greatest achievement was his teaching a doctrine of forgiveness, a quality totally unknown in Judaism. In the Our Father prayer[67] he invites us to pray "Forgive us our trespasses, as we forgive those that trespass against us". At face value the proposition appears quite straightforward — you will be forgiven for all your offences if you forgive everyone who has offended you. However the process is not quite so simple. Jesus said[68] "If you are offering your gift at the altar and there remember that your brother has something against you; leave your gift there at the altar. First go and be reconciled to your brother; then come and offer your gift." It is not sufficient for you to say "I forgive you" while perhaps enjoying a delicious feeling of moral superiority. Your responsibility is to repair your relationship so your brother feels OK about you, and there is peace in the community. Derrida[69] downgrades this process, calling it "conditional forgiveness" — forgiving where you hope to gain something by the transaction, as opposed to his concept of "true forgiveness" where there is no gain . . . and he goes on to say true forgiveness cannot exist because there is always gain for somebody. However it is important to discover what is gained, and by whom. The forgiveness advocated by Jesus is aligned with his ministry as it promotes harmony in the kingdom, so this could be called Christian forgiveness. In Judaism the concept of forgiveness did not exist, so up to Jesus' time, there was no possibility of forgiveness[70] for the Jewish people. They had a burden of guilt which they could not lay down, a burden which Jesus offered to set on his own shoulders. Now we have before us the prospect of the possibility of reconciliation: a lesson from a great Teacher which the world would do well to learn.

Jesus as Leader

As a leader Jesus established a community of followers, a kingdom not of the earth but nevertheless on the earth. David Jenkins, former Bishop of Durham, summed it up as "Of all the other-worldly religions, Christianity is the most this-worldly." This kingdom will be a just society where everyone serves, shares, and finds fulfillment. It is a kingdom on this earth, to be established in this life. He had little patience with those whose focus was on a perfect hereafter. Donald Reeves[71], former Rector of St. James Piccadilly, supported this view, rejecting the notion that the Church should be in any way divorced from politics, saying:

> "We are making connections between faith and life. People have reduced Christianity to going to church, but Jesus did not talk about the Church or even God, but about the Kingdom, about renewing every part of creation. If one was going to believe that the Church is the sole place where god is to be found, then God help the Church, and God help God."

We still have a long way to go. Jesus would find the present structure of our societies to be an abomination where wealth and power are the prerogatives of the few and the top 1% own over 90% of the substance of the world. In twenty centuries we still have not got it right. Jesus is with the atheists in this, sharing a concern for the here and now—as if there won't be a chance to fix it up later.

Jesus as Priest

As a priest Jesus preached a doctrine that was a combination of revolutionary action and personal contentment. This duality was represented in his teaching of the Lord's Prayer, a prayer is so simple, so perfect, it embraces all our duties and desires. Simone Weil[72] writes: "We cannot conceive of any prayer that is not already contained in it—it is to prayer what Christ is to humanity". If I were looking for proof of Christ's divinity I would not need to look any further than this.

Weil observed that of the six petitions in the Our Father the first three petitions are transcendent and the last three are immanent; that is, in the first three petitions praise and worship the universal Creator and in the last three we pray for our creaturely needs. The first three petitions contain the word "Thy"—Thy Name, Thy Kingdom, Thy Will . . . and the last three contain the word "Us"—feed us, forgive us, lead us. The first three deal with establishing the kingdom and the last three deal with our role in it. With Julian of Norwich, we should have faith "that all shall be well, and all shall be well, and all manner of thing shall be well." So we should be free of all anxiety, and trust that all shall be well, taking no heed for the morrow[73]: for the morrow can take care of itself. We should trust that the community we care for will in turn care for us. Jesus taught us to give thanks for the gifts we enjoy, to appreciate the way the earth supports us, and to render ourselves more extensively serviceable to our fellow creatures. He taught us to care for the world. Even though this world shall pass away we are its present custodians and he taught us that we should not shrink from doing what needs to be done to sustain the world, saying[74] "Courage, little flock; for it is your father's good pleasure to give you the kingdom."

How are we doing?—not very well. We are still in the mindset where our preoccupation with short-term profit and comfort trumps our interest in long-term survival, and that "long-term" could be pretty short. An economic engine, one that sterilizes the land and pollutes the air, rules the earth. Many of those opposing this process are so involved with the struggle they are distracted from noticing its most serious effects—how our pollution of the atmosphere is fouling the oceans that generate between 50% and 80% of the oxygen we breathe. The problem was outlined by Alanna Mitchell in her 2009 book[75] "Seasick". Mitchell explains how greenhouse gases from the burning of fossil fuels dissolve in the world's oceans and increase their acidity. This increased acidity inhibits the growth of corals which are hosts to plankton and other micro-organisms that combine carbon and calcium, releasing oxygen for us to breathe. The destruction of the corals is occurring at an increasing rate, and at some point present trends will extinguish them altogether (and us). These mass destructions have occurred in the past. Sixty-five million years ago a massive discontinuity destroyed the dinosaurs, and fifty-five million years ago a massive increase in world temperatures eliminated 75% of species. We are facing the possibility of a similar disaster, one of our own making, but we manage to avoid paying any attention to it. Carbon dioxide in the atmosphere has now reach 449 parts per million[76]. Before the industrial age, for the last 20 million years, that concentration had never exceeded 300 ppm.

Fig. 14. Perilous Procrastination

The human tendency to ignore the long-term effects of our actions was illustrated by the 4th Century Saint Augustine of Hippo[77], who was unwilling to forego the pleasures of immediate gratification in order to secure his long-term survival, saying "Lord, make me chaste and continent—but not yet!"

Our proclivity for thinking only in the short term is illustrated in a television commercial sponsored by the oil and gas industry. A masterful woman in a formal pant suit strides across the landscape and declares "America has enough natural gas reserves to last us a hundred years! Support American Energy!" Is this supposed to be good news, to reassure us? Does it not mean that in 101 years it's all gone? And all we have done with it is burn it.

A recent study predicts that all the coral will be gone in thirty-five years if we do nothing to prevent its destruction, but in fact we are adding to the problem, rushing breathlessly towards that tipping point at an increasing rate as the world builds more coal-fired plants at the rate of one a week. Reserves of coal, oil and gas are relics of a carbon-capture which occurred in the past on a vast scale, yet we are prepared to release this carbon back into the atmosphere. It is certain that if we extract all the fossil-fuels in *presently discovered* reserves—and new fields are still being sought every day—we will crash beyond any tipping point. The only solution is to leave these fuels in the ground—"Coal in the Hole, Oil in the Soil!". We are told the coal industry creates jobs; but what horrible dangerous jobs, grubbing around in the underground dark. Coal-mining is dangerous for the miners, and for everybody else. Coal is dirt cheap—that's the problem, it is that dirt that is slowly killing us. The coal-fired plants in Ohio are not only responsible for increased incidence of cancer in their immediate vicinity, prevailing winds dump this filth on Northern Ontario, on the pristine shores of Naiscoot Lake. Some religious fundamentalists are willfully blind to this possibility, or look to the future destruction of life on earth with equanimity, assured of profits in the short term followed by a rapture that will pluck them up to heaven while the rest of us get to expire in deserts as our just desserts. Perhaps the only evidence of our civilization that will survive will be our scientific creations in the fields of miniaturization, which could be of some use to the insects that will inherit the earth. I don't think this was Christ's vision for his Kingdom, but one day, one insect, being slightly more intelligent than the rest . . .

Jesus Reproaches

Jesus' reaction to the way his church evolved was recorded in a 9th Century poem "The Reproaches from the Cross". It forms part of some of the Good Friday liturgies. Here are a couple of verses . . .

> "O My people,
> What have I done to you?
> How have I offended you?
> > Answer Me!
> I have raised you up out of the prison house of sin and death,
> > and you have delivered up your Redeemer to be scourged.
> I have redeemed you from the house of bondage,
> > and you have nailed your Saviour to the cross.
> O My people,
> > Answer Me!
> "O My people,
> What have I done to you?
> How have I offended you?
> > Answer Me!
> > I gave you saving water from the rock,
> but you gave me gall and vinegar to drink.
> I gave you a royal scepter,
> but you gave me a crown of thorns.
> O My people,
> > Answer Me!"

Some sensitive souls have denounced this work as anti-semitic because it was addressed to the Jewish people. That was a strange charge because this address to the Jewish people was made by a Jewish prophet, and except for a Phoenician woman who asked for the crumbs under his table and a Roman centurion with a sick daughter, all his followers were Jewish.

Jesus Redux

If Jesus were to return to earth, not in his official role as The Second Coming but just on a tour of inspection to view the progress of his church, what would he say? Here is a conjecture . . .

> "O My people,
> How you have offended me!
> See what have you done to me!
> See what are you doing to me!
> > Answer Me!
> I gave you the keys to the kingdom
> And you have locked all the doors!
> I gave everything to the poor
> And you have robbed the poor for your own wealth!
> O My people, see what are you doing to me!
> > Answer Me!"

> "O My people,
> How you have offended me!
> See what have you done to me!
> See what are you doing to me!
> > Answer Me!
> I prayed in the wilderness
> But you need a palace for prayer!

I taught you to pray to Our Father
And now you pray to me!
O My people, see what are you doing to me!
       Answer Me!"

NOTES for Chapter Nine

[67] Matthew 6: 9
[68] Matthew 5: 23
[69] Jacques Derrida, On Cosmopolitanism and Forgiveness. 2001, New York, Routledge Kegan Paul.
[70] Mark 2: 7
[71] Stephanie Billen, quoted in a newspaper article in The Times (London), February 26, 1987.
[72] Simone Weil : Waiting on God, 1953, Routledge Kegan Paul, London
[73] Matthew 6: 34
[74] Luke 12:32
[75] Alanna Mitchell, Seasick. 2009, Toronto, McClelland and Stewart.
[76] European Environment Agency, Observed Trends in Global Concentrations of the Kyoto Gases, Feb 2015. National Oceanic and Atmospheric Administration
[77] St. Augustine of Hippo, Confessions VIII, 7 (*ca.* 397)

CHAPTER TEN
What Earthly Use Is Religion?

In the 1960's I came across the phrase by Carl Gustav Jung which forms the epigraph at the front of this book: "without religion modern man goes crazy." Notice that Jung is referring to religion, not faith. Faith can be solitary, but religion demands community. The word "religion" is derived from the Latin *religare*, meaning 'to bind', and refers to the obligations of reverence and ritual in a monastic community. In the OED religion is defined as "an organized system of beliefs, ceremonies, and rules used to worship a god, or a group of gods". One can participate in the rituals and obey the rules of such an organized system of beliefs without endorsing the beliefs themselves. It is possible to honor the spiritual connections implicit in a system of beliefs without necessarily accepting their substance.

Jung declared that a person needs to have spiritual connections in order to be healthy and well-rounded: to be aware of the Shadow, the Ego, the Other. Without such a spiritual connection "modern man" could indeed go crazy. These archetypes, if not perceived, could still be influencing his life in ways he might not realize if he were disconnected from his spiritual roots. Such connections are made in all the world's religions, in fraternities, in secret societies such as Freemasonry, in historic rituals, in Gothic novels, and in invocations of the Universal Mind. At that time, in the 1960's, my architectural firm had a staff of twenty-three, and when I considered the personality of each individual that was part of my team it was striking the way they fell into two groups.

Those who attended church or practiced meditation or yoga or had some other spiritual connection were in the main content, committed, happy and satisfied. Those who were of a solitary or materialist persuasion were angry, resentful, envious, and unfulfilled. The distinction was so obvious, so clear, I resolved to get some of that contentment for myself, but where should I look? I looked over all the available offerings, and it appeared that The Anglican Church of Canada (or the Episcopal Church in the US) would be the most congenial spiritual home, largely because it would make the fewest demands on me. I would not have to learn a new language, abstain from any sort of food or drink, wear strange clothes, grow a beard, undergo surgery, or submit to any undesirable intimacies.

When it came to my choosing a particular church I was already familiar with The Church of the Holy Trinity in downtown Toronto. The church operated a small café where they hosted poetry readings, and offered mid-week music recitals and lectures. The church was established in 1847 to be a church for the poor, "the seats to be free and unappropriated for ever"[78] This tradition of support for the underdog has run consistently through its history. The church has had City Councilors and Members of Parliament among its members, usually of a strong reform persuasion. Its members have been prominent in the Peace Movement, the Women's Movement, and the struggle for justice in Central and South America. At the time of the Viet Nam War hundreds of young people from the United States slept in the church, on their way to making a new life in Canada. The rear of the church was partitioned off to give the temporary residents a bit of privacy from the worshiping community, but this did not prevent the perfumes of illicit smoking mixtures from one side of the barrier from mingling with the incense from the other. The church provides offices for Amnesty International, for boycotts of various unacceptable products such as the canned milk being marketed by Nestlés to babies of the Third World, and a Distress Centre for suicide counseling

Fig. 15. The Church of the Holy Trinity, Toronto

These concerns filter into the worship of the community, which is strongly congregational in character. The liturgy is re-cast in inclusive language, which tempers some of the traditional imagery of masculine domination, so God is referred to at times as "our Father and Mother", continuing a tradition of the 5th Century Celtic church. This is one of the oldest churches in Toronto, but being in the commercial core of the city it has no surrounding residential community to enforce "community standards", so it is free to combine Anglo-Catholic high-church ritual with concern for the downtrodden and the marginalized.

Although the church is a listed historic building (see Fig. 15.) the pews were re-arranged to serve a centralized form of worship; but for the doubters and non-believers a grouping of armchairs was set up at the back, complete with newspapers, magazines and a coffee pot. That was the area to which I gravitated—if you want to protest the essential irrationality of religion you have to show up to do it—staying away won't cut it. However, after a few months I noticed that the people at the front of the church were having much more fun than I was, so I moved up to the front myself and joined the worshiping congregation. To my chagrin, nobody noticed!

What did the church offer me?

- An acknowledgement of the existence of the spiritual.
- Conversations that went beyond just being about making money or having fun.
- Historic continuity, and engagement in ancient rites.
- Beautiful language, music, architecture and ritual.
- Promoting the well-being of society by supporting social causes, charities, and political movements.
- An acknowledgement of excellence.
- A safe place for vulnerability and intimacy.
- New friendships with interesting people.

All this was available quite independently of one's religious beliefs. All churches have closet-atheists in their congregations, but at Holy Trinity that position would be respected. The church offered an uncritical welcome to all—priests having a crisis of faith, homeless people from the neighborhood, professors from York University, and members of the gay community that were not welcome in other churches which proclaimed the doctrine "love the sinner but hate the sin"—they hated the sin so much they would only accept the sinner if he had given up on it, although all the other sins were still permissible options.

This was not all plain sailing. The church came in for a lot of criticism for being a "sh*t-disturber", implying that the institutional church should not soil its hands with the excrement of society. At one point the church was threatened simultaneously with expropriation by the municipality and dis-establishment by the diocese. In all this turbulence the church attempted to carry on as a place of worship. The components of worship are thanksgivings, confessions, and intercessions.

We can all join in giving thanks for the wonders of the world around us. This does not imply subservience to some spiritual being. Gratitude is an appreciation for the joys in our lives, it does not imply indebtedness. If we feel we have to give thanks to a Creator for a beautiful sunset, that is where we should apply for a refund if the skies are grey. Most scientists are overawed with the wonder of the world they are studying, giving rise to Carl Sagan's observation[79] "Science is, at least in part, informed worship."

Confession is self examination, admitting our errors and omissions, the ways in which we have fallen short. Intercession is recognizing our creaturely needs and the needs of others. All this can take place without reference to a deity. The only item on the program that required belief was a recital of the Nicene Creed. This is not a prayer at all, it is a manifesto, a policy statement crafted in the 4th Century by a committee, and it sounds like it—a most inelegant piece of ancient writing, styled to ensure conformity and thwart the false doctrines of the Arians, Donatists, Nestorians, Gnostics, Marcionites and Manicheans. Although these threats have passed, when we recite the creed we are still manning the barricades to affirm how we would reject those false beliefs if we knew what they were. It's strange that so many of us take our own beliefs so seriously, yet we have no hesitation in inflicting beliefs we know to be spurious on young children.

Perhaps Santa Claus, the Tooth Fairy and the Easter Bunny have a value if they give children an insight into the delusional beliefs of adults. "Clap hands if you believe in fairies" is a creed, and like all the other creeds it relies on peer-pressure to ensure conformity. It also uses guilt: The statement[80] "Every time you say you don't believe in fairies, a fairy dies." is in the same vein as the guilt we are supposed to share for the execution by the state of a troublesome itinerant preacher two thousand years ago. When I'm invited to participate in communal guilt with the question "Were you there when they crucified my Lord?" the reply is "Of course not! I wasn't even born at the time!"

I Believe . . .

At the Church of the Holy Trinity the Creed which is intended to unify the congregation was the one item where we all had different responses. Some of us were obedient and believed it, others didn't believe it but recited it anyway, some recited an edited version, some invoked the Christian symbol of the cross in the disposition of their fingers, some just mumbled it and some were silent. However we were careful not to give offence nor to disturb the flow of the liturgy with personal redactions. My own version of the creed was "I believe—*mumble-mumble*—he suffered under Pontius Pilate, was crucified, died and was buried.—*mumble mumble*—Amen."—sounds like an obituary notice for the historical Jesus. Strangely, we found a unity in our rejection of a blanket interpretation.

That church was a great learning experience but I would not say that being there was comfortable or easy—if you were feeling down or a bit fragile Holy Trinity was the place to stay away from—the intellectual rigor was confronting. However that strange church served us for many years until we had children. At that point there were only four children enrolled in the Children's Program (two of them ours) so we felt the need to look for a more family-oriented institution. We settled on a very different church—well organized, bright-and-cheerful, and totally predictable, with a responsibly-supervised program for the children. However I missed the creative chaos of Holy Trinity, so I gravitated to the chapel at Trinity College which offers a variety of experiences ranging from a traditional Evensong with Mags and Nuncs beautifully voiced by a celestial choir, a weekly community eucharist followed by a community meal, historic re-enactments of ancient liturgies, Taizé gatherings, and an informal early-morning Mass on Fridays for a permanent congregation of students, staff, alumni, and people who had walked in off the street. This assembly became my parish church.

Congregations require consensus in order to cohere. This consensus need not be an undertaking to adopt a set of beliefs, although for some congregations that could be a requirement. For other congregations it might be sufficient for the congregation to have a consensus about its *attitudes* to belief. Some churches could accept any individual as leader regardless of his/her religious beliefs, or lack of them, as long as the liturgy was led in an approved manner. Jim Fisk, the Rector of The Church of the Holy Trinity in Toronto, said "Anyone who walks in through the doors here is a member of this church." For such a church to function there has to be agreement to let the liturgy follow its appointed course despite any personal reservations of any individuals. This was illustrated at the same church when a visitor objected to small children sharing in the bread and wine ("Careful now! Just a sip! Not too much!") saying we were on a path to damnation. Canon Ken Maxted reprimanded him, saying "We are all very tolerant here. If you are not going to be tolerant too you should leave! Now!"

For the liturgy to function the leader must lead from the centre, so the priest does not have the luxury of expressing his personal views. Two priests have told me what a burden this is, not to be able to discuss any doubts or share any reservations they might have. At their ordinations[81], many years ago, each one undertook . . .

" . . . to be ready, with all faithful diligence, to banish and drive away all erroneous and strange doctrines contrary to God's Word [as defined by the Bishop] and to use both public and private monitions and exhortations as need shall require and occasion shall be given", and

" . . . to reverently obey the Ordinary and other chief Ministers unto whom is committed charge and government, following with a glad mind and will their godly admonitions, and submitting to their godly judgements."

In the interval since their ordination they had acquired their own "godly judgments" and they found it a great burden not to be able to disclose them. They found it increasingly difficult to preserve "a glad mind and will" while professing what they did not believe, while the costs of public confession would be huge: family having to move out of the rectory, being unemployable in any diocese south of the Arctic Circle, breaking up a lot of friendships, and even being subject to scorn, as Bill Phipps found out. Bill was the Moderator of the United Church of Canada in 1976. The United Church was founded in 1925 by a union of the Methodist and Presbyterian churches, and it was expected that the leader would lead from the centre; that's why he was called the Moderator. After years of theological studies Bill came to a personal realization that beliefs in Jesus' virgin birth and his eventual resurrection were not necessary for salvation. When he disclosed this opinion there was outrage;

not from members of his church, and not from his superiors (he was the boss so he didn't have superiors) but from the Toronto Sun, a tabloid newspaper. His disgrace made headlines. It was plastered all over the front page of the Sun, the back page being reserved for the provocative charms of the SUNshine Girl. Bold headlines denounced his apostasy! It was a scandal, an affront! Even if the membership of the United Church of Canada were OK with the revelation the readers of the Toronto Sun were not, as attested to by letters to the editor that followed. It was hard to understand their anger, and I am wondering if this book might not spark a similar reaction from those who have not examined the subject. From my own experience I have noticed that the more I study theology (and I have over a thousand books on the subject) the more its doctrines appear to be the result of political expedience rather than divine revelation. In this respect religion is like a good single malt—both have aspects of the divine but both are essentially manufactured items; and results could be unfortunate if you indulge to excess in either of them.

There is a long tradition for religious thought to be presented in two versions: as a rigorous and enquiring study for theologians and a more simple-minded and romantic version for the general public. Five thousand years ago the Egyptians adopted a religion inherited from the Sumerians, based on the movements of the stars in the heavens. This stellar religion was cool and intellectual. It was studied intensely by the priesthood, but it had little appeal for the general population so a more immediate solar religion was created, and the two existed in parallel. The Sumerians were expert astronomers. They had discovered that the axis for the rotation of the earth does not maintain a constant angle relative to the solar system but has a slight wobble, as may be seen in a spinning top as it slows down. They calculated that the axis of the earth takes 25,920 years to make one revolution of wobble, what we call The Precession of the Equinoxes. There is a record of Pythagoras voyaging to Alexandria to learn The Great Year of the Egyptians. The value the Sumerians observed for the periodicity was close to what we can measure today with our sophisticated instruments—a wonderful achievement.

The Sumerians also had the ability to predict solar eclipses, and this gave the priesthood a powerful tool for controlling the population. They would say "Ra, the Sun God, is very angry with your backsliding and, unless you shape up, in 37 days he is going to take off in his chariot and all your crops will fail!" and sure enough, at the appointed time all the birds would stop singing and the sky would darken and the sun would start to disappear, and the people would rush to re-affirm their undertakings—a sort of involuntary Confirmation Class. This duality, having one doctrine for public consumption and a separate one for private enlightenment, generated great stability for a regime that lasted unchanged for more than a thousand years.

This duality persists to the present day. Some theologians accept it's existence and some reject it. St. Ignatius was one of the hard-liners. In his "Spiritual Exercises" of 1552[82] he demands total conformity to the doctrines of Rome, saying

> "We must put aside all judgment of our own. If we wish to proceed securely in all things we must first hold fast to the following principle: What seems to me white I will believe to be black if the hierarchical church so defines!".

This security comes at a terrible cost, setting a standard which many found it impossible to achieve, and many suffered consequent guilt for their failures. Jesus did not demand that we abandon all initiative and intelligence in order to follow him. He explained this in his parable of The Wicked Servant[83] who was so afraid of losing his master's money he buried it in a hole in the ground instead of investing it.

The Council of Trent, a Roman Catholic enclave, took a more liberal view. Here's the Tridentine Decree from the twenty-fifth Council Session that met in 1596:

> "Let the more difficult and subtle questions, and those which tend not to edification, and seldom contribute aught to piety, be kept back from popular discourses among the uneducated vulgar. Neither let them suffer the public mention and treatment of uncertain points, or such as look like falsehood. But those things which tend to a certain kind of curiosity or superstition. or which savor of filthy lucre, let them prohibit as scandals and stumbling blocks to the faithful."

Fifty years after that decree, in 1650, the Anglican Bishop John Bramhall[84] could write that no one was required to believe the Thirty-Nine Articles of Religion, only not to teach otherwise. Thus we can see a situation where, although it would not be possible, with integrity, for an atheist to be ordained as a priest because that involves a public statement regarding one's beliefs, it might transpire that over time such a priest could develop into becoming an atheist, and that would be permissible as long as his or her private and public avocations were kept separate. Some can accomplish this easier than others. Some may become more effective ministers of religion if they cease being people of faith—they could gain an insight into the complexities of the lives of others by observing their own inconsistencies. Studying theology for some reinforces faith, while for others it raises doubts. For some priests becoming an atheist is a spiritual crisis; for others it could be blessed relief. The more one studies theology the more one realizes that all religions are human constructs, and those constructing them might have hidden motives.

Doing Good

Religion has often been regarded as a repository of all that is noble and moral, a reflection of man's finest instincts, a bulwark against the forces of evil; this despite the fact that many crimes and cruelties have been committed in its name. With this mindset it is possible to regard atheists, those who do not endorse its pleadings, as being unpredictable, untrustworthy, and possibly evil. We tend to fear those we do not understand. Part of the problem is statistical—there appear to be many Christians and very few atheists. The umbrella term "Christian" is well understood. This umbrella shelters a huge number of philosophies and beliefs ranging from TV evangelists to desert-dwelling anchorites, from the farm families of Mennonites to celibate Jesuits, from austere Quakers to Holy Rollers, from prosperous industrialists to the Poor Clares. The umbrella is huge, but many sheltering under it do not recognize one another. In contrast, there is no convenient umbrella term for those who doubt the existence of god. These may describe themselves (arranged alphabetically) as

    Antitheists
    Atheists
    Christian Atheists
    Doubters
    Empiricists
    Free-thinkers
    Humanists
    Igtheists
    Irreligious
    Logical positivists
    N/A
    Non-believers

No-religion
Rationalists

These do not shelter under an overall umbrella, which would make them easy to relate to—they represent dozens of individual umbrellas, and for protection some of them hide under their umbrellas. They have many options for how they will fill in the "RELIGION?" box on a census form. If I had been asked to respond to such a query I would have said "Anglican", seeing no conflict between being Anglican and Atheist. However if the question were "What do you believe?" my response would be "None of your business!" With this range of descriptors, overlapping definitions, and the lack of any overall organization atheists are difficult to recognize. Consequently they are The Stranger, and strangers are unpredictable and perhaps dangerous. Because they are unfamiliar to most people they are not trusted, and it has been said that in the United States (and possibly Canada) it would be impossible for any self-proclaimed atheist to be elected to any government office. When he was the presidential nominee for the Republican Party former President George H.W. Bush[85] was reported as saying:

> "No, I don't know that Atheists should be considered as citizens, nor should they be considered as patriots. This is one nation under God."

In this remark he was articulating the unease felt by many Americans at the prospect of any atheist having a role in the running of the country. We know that all religions have laws so the adherents of religions are expected to have at least an appearance of being law-abiding. For Jews there is a consensus that there are either 10 or 613 laws, for Christians it is 2 or 10, and for Anglicans there are perhaps an additional 39. Atheists are not bound by any of these laws, so there is always the threat that atheists might not be law-abiding. However, most atheists would agree with Socrates that a framework of laws is necessary for the smooth functioning of society and should be obeyed, although not all would take obedience to the extreme that he did.

Christian Atheists

Is it possible for an atheist to be a Christian? It depends on who you ask. There are many Christian denominations with their own code of beliefs, so there would be many different answers. Is it possible to follow the teachings of Jesus without adopting a belief system? And if so, could those without a belief system be called Christians? These seem to be reasonable assumptions, generating the possibility for atheists to be Christian. Some denominations might deny that, but I am not prepared to yield to them the right to decide the issue for me. I do not accept that they have any jurisdiction outside their own membership. Thomas Jefferson took a similar stand, saying:

> "To the corruptions of Christianity I am indeed opposed, but not to the genuine precepts of Jesus himself. I am a Christian in the only sense he wished anyone to be: sincerely attached to his doctrines in preference to all others."

He would accept the three roles for Jesus as set out in Chapter 9, those of Teacher, Leader, and Priest; and in accepting those roles would come to know Jesus as Friend.

Christians, even atheist Christians, are required to worship in community, to bring forth the Kingdom. What would such a church have to offer? Substantially it would have to be a list similar to that listing of qualities that induced me to join The Church of the Holy Trinity, where atheists were as welcome as anybody else. The list is:

- An acknowledgement of the existence of the spiritual.
- Conversations that go beyond being about making money or having fun.

- Historic continuity, and engagement in ancient rites.
- Beautiful language, music, architecture and ritual.
- Promoting the well-being of society by supporting social causes.
- An acknowledgement of excellence.
- A safe place for vulnerability and intimacy.
- New friendships with interesting people.

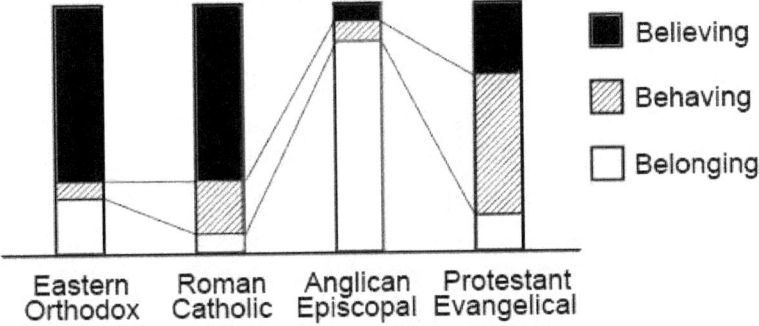

Fig. 16. Characteristics of various Christian Denominations.

The ministry of the church can be seen as a combination of believing, behaving, and belonging. How do the various religious denominations shape up? The chart in Fig. 16 plots the distribution of the importance of these qualities among the various denominations, taking as a baseline an equal distribution for the three of them in the ministry of Jesus. Reginald Bibby[86] has made statistical studies of attitudes to these qualities under the headings of attendance, identification, and belief. The Orthodox and Roman churches set a high premium on belief. These churches impose dogma with authoritarian statements — the Roman church even pronounces some of its doctrinal statements as infallible. Concerning the other qualities, the Orthodox churches, representing nations with a range of languages, achieve unity by focusing on communities, which is classified as "belonging". In contrast the Roman church for most of its history has enforced a single language, Ecclesiastical Latin, so "belonging" is taken for granted. The Roman church operates with a cycle of sin-confession-absolution-penance and sin-again, so its secondary preoccupation is with "behaving".

For the Anglican church it is considered impolite to enquire after anybody's beliefs or behavior, so for this church "belonging" is the prime social organizer, in fact it could be said that the Anglican/Episcopal church is a social club that also conducts worship services.

For the Protestant/Evangelical churches belonging is only extended to those with suitable beliefs and behaviors, with behavior being dominant. Some of these churches where preaching is prime have huge congregations that number in the thousands. Here it isn't possible to experience the intimacy that creates for a community a sense of belonging. The gathering is essentially an audience that will disperse after the performance. The lack of community and personal involvement in those huge mega-churches leads to a falling away of individual attendance, often to once or twice a month—or less. Scott Thumma[87], director of the Hartford Institute for Religion Research, notes that "They think 'regular attendance' is 'I get there when I can.' "

Of all the various communions it appears that it is the Anglican/Episcopal church that offers the most congenial accommodation for the atheist. Here nobody is required to believe anything, just not to interfere with the beliefs of others. There is a possibility for participating in a rich heritage of language and music. All the trappings of tradition are here, where they can be enjoyed without the burden of commitment. Across the centuries both Ralph Waldo Emerson and Richard Dawkins had an appreciation for the ambience of worship without endorsing its content. Emerson[88] said "I like the silent church before the service begins, better than any preaching." And Dawkins[89] remarked : " I suppose I'm a cultural Anglican, and I see evensong in a country church through much the same eyes as I see a village cricket match on the village green. I have a certain love for it."

Robin Williams' Top 10 Reasons to be an Episcopalian

10. No snake handling.
9. You can believe in dinosaurs.
8. Male and female God created them; male and female we ordain them.
7. You don't have to check your brains at the door.
6. Pew aerobics.
5. Church year is color-coded.
4. Free wine on Sunday.
3. All of the pageantry—none of the guilt.
2. You don't have to know how to swim to get baptized.

and the Number One reason to be an Episcopalian:

1. No matter what you believe, there's bound to be at least one other Episcopalian who agrees with you.

Fig.17. Database for the Episcopal Church

Robin Williams[90] made a similar choice to join the Episcopal Church—he became a member of the congregation of St. Augustine by-the-Sea Episcopal Church in Santa Monica, California, and he published his rationale in the parish magazine: see Fig.17.

George Bernard Shaw is quoted as saying "I am an atheist, and I thank God for it!" It's probable he could find within the Anglican/Episcopal church a sympathetic environment where he could express his gratitude for being so blessed. The church already extends a warm welcome for members of CA-CA, the Communion of Anglo-Catholic Atheists.

At first sight it seems ironic that the church which puts the highest premium on believing—the Roman Catholic church—is also the denomination which in North America has the greatest component (32%) of those who are not believers. The canonical beliefs become less acceptable when one reflects on the financial and political motivations of those proposing these beliefs. Some of the required beliefs are merely sentimental, and some are totally irrational, such as the churches teaching on contraception which has the power to overcrowd the globe to the point of extinction within a few generations if allowed to proceed unchecked. Many of those wishing to remain in the church reject in private what they have to affirm in public.

In contrast, it is the Anglican/Episcopal church that makes the lowest demands for conformity of belief. This was outlined by Robin Williams "You don't have to check your brains at the door". Here Atheists will find an easy welcome into a religious community where they will be able to find others who think as they do.

NOTES for Chapter Ten

[78] Eric Arthur, Toronto, No Mean City. 1964. Oxford University Press.
[79] Carl Sagan, Varieties of Scientific Experience. 2006, Penguin.
[80] J.M. Barrie, Peter Pan , or the Boy who wouldn't Grow Up. 1904 play.
[81] The Book of Common Prayer according to the use of The Anglican Church of Canada, 1959. The Ordering of Priests.
[82] The Spiritual Exercises of St. Ignatius 1968 Loyola Press.
[83] Matthew 25:14.
[84] Paul Gibson, Discerning the Word, 2000. Anglican Book Centre, Toronto.
[85] Robert I. Sherman, reporting on a public press conference at O'Hare Airport, August 27, 1987.
[86] Reginald W. Bibby, Beyond the Gods and Back, 2011, Lethbridge AB, A Project Canada Book.
[87] Cathy Lynn Grossman: December 2, 2015 Religion News Service
[88] Ralph Waldo Emerson, Self-Reliance and Other Essays
[89] Richard Dawkins, in The Spectator magazine, September 14, 2013.
[90] Robin Williams in Ebb&Flow, November 2002 Parish Magazine, St. Augustine by-the-Sea Episcopal Church, Santa Monica, CA

CHAPTER ELEVEN
Agony of the Agnostics

In the Oxford English Dictionary an agnostic is defined as "a person who believes that nothing is known or can be known of the existence or nature of God." In the corresponding Merriam Webster Dictionary an agnostic is "a person who neither believes nor disbelieves in the existence of a deity or deities; a person who does not have a definite belief about whether God exists or not." The Merriam Webster definition needs expansion. One cannot simultaneously believe and disbelieve something. Surely that definition means that the agnostic believes that God may or may not exist. The word agnostic derives from the Ancient Greek α (a), meaning "without", and γνωσις (gnōsis), meaning knowledge, and is usually taken to mean that an agnostic is one who professes to have no knowledge of whether God exists or not, or believes that it is not possible for a human to have such knowledge.

Agnostics present themselves, and wish to be perceived by others, as taking a middle way between the towering structures of belief erected by people of faith and the atheists' empty landscape of doubt. This commonly-accepted structure is illustrated in Fig. 18, which tabulates popular perceptions, and shows agnostics as occupying a middle ground between people of faith and atheists. However the definitions of agnostic in both the dictionaries quoted above contain the word "belief", and those beliefs are in opposition to the beliefs of people of faith. Thus a logical structure would put atheists

POPULAR PERCEPTIONS OF BELIEVERS AND ATHEISTS			
	PEOPLE OF FAITH	AGNOSTICS	ATHEISTS
Typical quotes	"I know I am right"	"You may very well be right"	"Show me"
Popular description	Old-fashioned	Doesn't know what to believe.	Doesn't believe in God.
Perceived character	Closed minded	Wishy-washy	Argumentative, rude
Assumed Personality	Judgmental	Chicken	Arrogant
Ultimate Outcome	State Religion	Chaos	Communism

Fig, 18. Tabulation of popular perceptions and comments on believers and atheists.

in the central column as in Fig. 19, flanked by those who believe that they know a God that exists and those that believe we cannot know whether God exists. Those beliefs are both permanent beliefs, as defined in Chapter Three, but they are focused in opposite directions. They are permanent beliefs because they are not based on observation, so no new evidence can temper them. In contrast the atheist observes that, as yet, no evidence has come forward to prove the existence of God. This is a working hypothesis, what I call a

	LOGICAL DISTINCTIONS		
	PEOPLE OF FAITH	ATHEISTS	AGNOSTICS
Core Beliefs	Believe that knowledge of God is possible, and "We have it."	Observe that up to now there is no evidence for the existence of God, or gods.	Believe that knowledge of God or gods is not possible for humankind.
Class of Belief	Permanent	Provisional	Permanent

Fig. 19. Tabulation of logical distinctions between People of Faith, Atheists, and Agnostics.

provisional belief that is subject to revision when new evidence presents itself. Atheists and agnostics see no proof or evidence for the existence of God; but despite this lack of evidence agnostics shy away from deducing that there is no God, saying it is not possible for humans to know this with certainty. Agnostics are not uncommitted atheists, they are indecisive people of faith. Laurence Brown[91] of the University of New South Wales poses the question to agnostics, "You claim that nothing can be known with certainty... how, then, can you be so sure?" Saying that God is unknowable is making a profound statement of a theological belief. People of faith and agnostics are believers but their beliefs are diametrically opposite, so it is logical to place atheists who subscribe to neither of these beliefs in the central column of the tabulation of Fig 18.

Russell's Teapot

Bertrand Russell illustrated the idiocy of making a statement which contains its own antithesis by asking us to consider a teapot[92] ...

> "If I were to suggest that between the Earth and Mars there is a china teapot revolving about the sun in an elliptical orbit, nobody would be able to disprove my assertion provided I were careful to add that the teapot is too small to be revealed even by our most powerful telescopes.
>
> "But if I were to go on to say that, since my assertion cannot be disproved, it is an intolerable presumption on the part of human reason to doubt it, I should rightly be thought to be talking nonsense."

This is essentially the position of the agnostic who says that because no proof exists that says god does not exist we must assume the possibility that god may exist. The fallacy of this argument is that it can be applied equally well to orbiting teapots and anything else we might consider, and for which there is no evidence. However there is a positive side to the argument: it disposes of mythical UFO's. If there were no flying teapots there would be no purpose for orbiting teacups which would eliminate a need for flying saucers. How could such a daft idea that defies all logic and experience originate? Russell goes on to say:

> "If, however, the existence of such a teapot were affirmed in ancient books, taught as the sacred truth every Sunday, and instilled into the minds of children at school, hesitation to believe in its existence would become a mark of eccentricity and entitle the doubter

to the attentions of the psychiatrist in an enlightened age or of the Inquisitor in an earlier time."

Schrödinger's Pets

In 1935 Erwin Schrödinger, an Austrian physicist, used the example of a cat-in-a-box to illustrate quantum theory. In addition to the cat the box contains some scientific equipment by which a poison fatal to the cat would be released if a particle should be emitted by a radioactive substance.

Fig. 20. Schrödinger's kitten—now you see it, then you didn't.

Was the particle emitted? That is the same question as asking "Did the cat survive?" Without opening the box your guess is as good as mine. Perhaps yes, perhaps no—we can't reach a definite answer, we can only assess probabilities.

It's not generally known that Schrödinger's cat had kittens (so I guess it survived). I built a playhouse for one of them out of a discarded carton (See Fig.20). It's a box with two compartments that are separated by a partition which has a hole in it. Each compartment has its own lid. I put Schrödinger's kitten in one of the compartments and closed both lids. Which compartment contains the kitten? To check I opened the right-hand lid and there's no kitten; but it's possible that by my opening the lid I had scared her and she bolted through the hole and hid in the other compartment. And if I'd found the kitten she might have been attracted by the prospect of escape and come through from the other side. Could it be that the act of looking for the kitten determined its whereabouts. So where was it before I started looking for it?

We can only infer probabilities. This gives new meaning to the phrase "Seek and ye shall find!" By seeking we may create what we find. To seek god we first have to have found him. Schrödinger's kitten is a quantum cat.

Schrödinger also had a dog. Here's the story: UPS leaves a box outside the door of the person-of-faith. There's no address on it, just a label saying "This Package Contains One China Schrödinger Dog—Handle with Care". (Hint: DOG is GÖD spelled backwards, and may be discovered in a crumbling RC SHRINE.) The person-of-faith is delighted to receive this; it's what he's always wanted, and in order to be sure not to damage the contents he does not open the box but puts the whole package in his china cabinet where he can admire it.

UPS leaves a box outside the door of the agnostic. There's no address on it, just a label saying "This Package Contains One China Schrödinger Dog—Handle with Care". The agnostic does not know whether the package is intended for him, or whether there is in fact anything in it, so he leaves it on the doorstep. Next day he finds a package on his doorstep. He does not know whether it is the same package as before, or a replacement.

UPS leaves a box outside the door of the atheist. There's no address on it, just a label saying "This Package Contains One China Schrödinger Dog—Handle with Care". The atheist opens the box, finds nothing in it, so he flattens the box and puts it in the recycling bin where there are dozens of other flattened packages of various sizes with labels saying "This Package Contains One China Schrödinger Dog—Handle with Care".

Agnostic Agonies

"Agnostic" means ignorant; it means (literally) "without knowledge". That is a condition that most people would prefer not to disclose if it applied to themselves, so why do agnostics wear their ignorance as a badge of honor? Are they so are afraid of insulting any residual God by doubting his existence that they shy away from the conversation? Or are they attempting to avoid all conflict with others by having no position of their own, perhaps not realizing that by sitting on the fence they are potential targets to those on both sides. They make self-referencing statements that say they are not making a statement or their position is one of not adopting a position. By this means they disengage from the conversation. That would be fine with me as long as it were true, but it's not. They go on talking about it. They go on at length about how accepting they are, how tolerant and respectful of all faiths, and they even go so far as to respect those with none. Thanks! H.L. Mencken put some limits on tolerance, saying "We must respect the other fellow's religion, but only in the sense and to the extent that we respect his theory that his wife is beautiful and his children smart." Ezra Pound[93] was more forthright, saying "To bow down to gods not one's own is flattery, bigosh!"

The blanket acceptance in public of what is rejected in private is a feature of multiculturalism, which comes to a head in interfaith services where all the religious institutions in an area come together for shared worship. Like all interfaith dialogues they are in fact serial monologues, with no shared theology to unify them.

Those who wish to be conciliatory at all costs, and avoid making any critical remarks, may find themselves making some strange endorsements, such as those parodied by Noel Coward in his 1943 wartime song

> "Don't let's be beastly to the Germans
> For they're civilized when all is said and done
> Let's be meek to them
> And turn the other cheek to them
> But don't let's be beastly to the Hun."

Agnostics are preoccupied with political correctness, with not giving offence to anyone's religious proclivities, which explains why so many people find their weak-kneed subservience offensive. While the person-of-faith is parked in the past, and the atheist is driving ahead into a future, the indecisive AGNOSTIC is just COASTING.

NOTES for Chapter Eleven

[91] Laurence B. Brown, MisGod'ed: A Roadmap of Guidance and Misguidance in the Abrahamic Religions, 2008. CreateSpace Ind.
[92] Bertrand Russell, Is There a God? 1952. Commissioned but not published by Illustrated Magazine.
[93] Ezra Pound, The Pisan Cantos. 1945, London, Faber & Faber.

CHAPTER TWELVE

Can Atheists save the Church?

Well, people of faith haven't been doing such a great job, so perhaps it is time for atheists to give it a shot. Faith might be able to move mountains but it has not been so effective in filling the pews.

In most churches attendance is down, and many are closing down altogether. It's a constant matter of concern for episcopal discussion groups. They are trying many things: parish picnics, men's groups, bible study, children's programs, book clubs, retreats, youth camps, film nights, pancake breakfasts, church suppers, the internet, choral concerts—none of it seems to be working, and some of the measures are counter-productive, such as projecting the words of the hymns on video screens so we can get rid of the hymn books and impress young people with our hi-tech savvy. This is hardly cutting edge technology, it is not going to gain young people's respect, and a recent study by Deloitte[94] indicates that for young Millennials, that is people born between 1981 and 2000, there is an overwhelming preference for print books over e-books, and they are willing to pay for them rather than pirate them on-line or borrow them from a library. They enjoy the physical presence and heft of paper, ink and cardboard, as opposed to absorbing the flickering pixels on a screen. So it's not a good idea for us to hang screens in the chancel and invest in a lot of AV equipment; that train has already left the station.

The one thing that receives no attention, and the one thing that only the church can offer, is worship. All the churches problems would be solved if worship became an exciting engaging experience that would draw in the crowds, but it's not. It never was! We can look back with nostalgia to the days when churches were filled to capacity and congregations were expanding. In those days churches were full, but I'm not sure there were any more real worshipers then than we have today. Most of the people who showed up for church in those days did so because there was nothing else to do on a Sunday. When I first came to Canada I arrived on a Sunday and all the stores were closed. The local department stores had drapes drawn across their windows so passers-by would not be distracted from their devotions. Swings and teeter-totters in public parks were chained up so small children would not be tempted by these secular attractions. There was no Sunday shopping, you couldn't get a drink, no theatre or film shows, no alternative to going to church. It gave the phrase "Being driven to church" a new meaning. It's what everybody did, the lowest common denominator.

Before we start to mourn the passing of a golden age of church attendance I think we should consider what was taking place in the church. Most of those attending were not there for worship, they were showing up as a result of social pressure or because on a Sunday there was nothing else to do. We cannot look back at those years and say that large attendances showed that worship was popular in those days; and that the liturgy had a perfection that we should attempt to emulate today. It was not perfect in those days, and the vast crowds that showed up were not attracted by the liturgy, they came to get out of the house, to get dressed up, and to meet and have conversations with friends. The true predominant religion, at least in Canada at that time, was not Christianity: it was "churchgoing".

In earlier times attendance was even more strictly enforced. In Calvin's church in Geneva one of the duties of the

Deacon was to take attendance, and if a member did not show up on a Sunday the Deacon would visit his home on the Monday, and if the absentee did not have a sufficiently good excuse he would have to present himself at the church for judgment. In his "Ecclesiastical Ordinances of Geneva"[95] Calvin writes

> "If anyone is negligent in attending worship so a noticeable offense is evident for the communion of the faithful, or if anyone shows himself contemptuous of ecclesiastical discipline, he is to be admonished. If he becomes obedient he is to be dismissed in love. If he persists, passing from bad to worse, after having been admonished three times, he is to be excommunicated and denounced to the magistrate."

In a similar vein, when a student at my son's school informed the Headmaster that he should be excused from attending Chapel because "he did not believe in God," the Headmaster replied "The only thing you have to believe here is that attendance at Chapel is compulsory."

There is another problem. Most churches are really not suitable for worship. Most churches have adopted a traditional layout, but that tradition is comparatively recent. It was in the 1820's that the Cambridge Camden Society, a group of intellectuals and aesthetes at Cambridge University sought to recover an ancient piety by resurrecting an ancient form of church building. They could have chosen the form of the early Christian churches, a single space where the people gather around a central altar, but it was unfortunate that they opted for something much more theatrical and chose to follow a monastic model. True, it was ancient, but in that particular set-up the people had very little involvement. Monks were required to gather for worship up to eight times a day for Matins, Lauds, Prime, Terce, Sext, None, Vespers and Compline. For this they assembled in the Choir, a room with facing choir stalls and an altar at the east end. The choir was not reserved for those monks with the best voices, all the monks were required to chant all the prayers. An open room was built on to the west end of the choir where the townspeople could come and observe the monks' devotions but there was no question of their being allowed to participate. Probably they would not have been able to anyway because the worship was all in Latin. The people did not worship in this situation, they were being allowed to witness the worship of others.

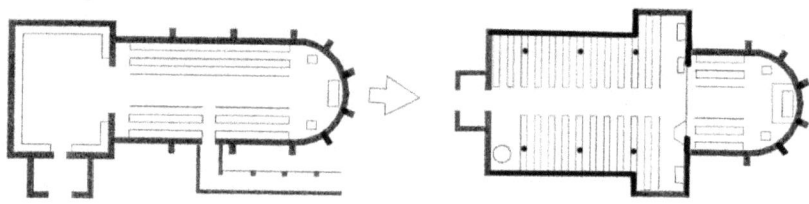

Fig. 21. In 1820 the Cambridge Camden Society adopted a plan that was typical for a monastery chapel (left) and adapted it to create the church layout we now regard as traditional (right).

It was this arrangement that morphed into the plan for what we now call the traditional church, and virtually all churches built after 1820 adopted this plan. The monk's choir becomes the chancel which retains the same inward-facing seating arrangement, and the nave expands and lengthens to accommodate larger crowds. The plan also perpetuates another tradition: it does little to encourage participation by the people. They sit on wooden benches arranged in parallel rows on a flat floor, and through an archway they can see (or rather, those in the front few rows can see, the rest can see only the backs of people's heads) a raised chancel where a robed choir occupies inward facing stalls, and beyond that, up still more steps and behind a fence an altar is set against the end wall. The chancel would be brightly lit, in fact one of the requirements of the Cambridge Camden Society was that the lighting in the nave should be kept dim[96] to enhance the feeling of being present at a sacred mystery.

Christians are required to worship in community; and worship is very different from private prayer, but how much community can you feel if all you can see in front of you is the backs of people's heads? Can we expect people to come and worship with us when we offer them a hard seat where they cannot see anything and perhaps cannot hear much either. In even the humblest hockey arena in rural Ontario the seating is better than this—at least, everybody can see all the ice—so is it reasonable to expect visitors will wish to enroll in a church that offers such sub-standard facilities?

Churches find it very difficult to deal with this situation. The problem is that after the congregational exodus most of the survivors fall into two categories; both of them ineffective. On the one hand there are the people-of-faith. They probably feel they can worship anywhere and their surroundings are not important to them so they see no need to make any adjustment to them. On the other hand there are those who revere the institutional church with all its pomp and ceremony, and this group does not want to change anything. They want to keep everything "as it was in the beginning", not realizing how recent that beginning was. These groups who stay with the church after most of the membership has left realize that they have a problem: that with such a small congregation the church is no longer financially sustainable, that the givings are inadequate to support its ministry, that at some point its endowments are going to run out, and meanwhile picnics and pancakes are not solving the problem.

Can atheists save the church? I think it is the only solution. If I were a person of faith I think I would find it very difficult to take a chain-saw to the altar if that were what was required. It is just too difficult for people of faith to be objective about their situation when they have such a strong subjective attachment to it—all they can offer is minor tweaking in the hope that it will work, and it never does. They have been careful to use only acceptable stones for their temple, but it is the stone that the builders rejected, the outcast, that must provide the foundation for the new temple if it is going to stand firm against new forces surrounding it.

When a congregation with a traditional worship space has been sufficiently perceptive (or sufficiently desperate) to engage me as a Liturgical Consultant the solutions I offer have always been far more radical than anything they had previously considered, yet when it comes to a vote they have always been accepted by a margin of at least 95%, sometimes unanimously, because I point out to them how their worship can be aligned with ancient Christian traditions springing from the early church, and how the individual worshiper is respected. They perceive a future that will be more engaging than anything they could ask for or imagine, and this fills them with enthusiasm and joy.

For Christian worship to be an engaging experience some criteria have to be met:
    1. The space must express welcome.
    2. Everybody has to be able to see everything.
    3. Everybody has to be able to hear and participate in what is sung and spoken.
    4. The communion table is to be the focus of the space.
    5. Seating must be arranged to express "community", rather than "audience".

You can see that none of these requirements are met in a church of "traditional" style so why are we surprised when people choose not to attend, choose to have other priorities and seek other pursuits? And why do we think (or at least hope) that a superficial tinkering[97] will solve anything? We have a radical (springing from the root) problem, and this requires a radical solution. Perhaps a radical solution requires a radical agent, and the radical agent for this role could be one who has some skills, who loves the church, and is an Atheist. The *Te Deum Laudamus,* a 4th Century hymn of praise, proclaims that Christ "has opened the Kingdom of Heaven to all believers[98]" — fair enough. However to set up his Kingdom on Earth he could perhaps benefit from a bit of help from those who do not believe.

NOTES for Chapter Twelve

[94] Duncan Stewart, TMT Research Bulletin 2015, Deloitte Canada.
[95] John Calvin, Ecclesiastical Ordinances, 1541. tr G.R. Potter and M. Greengrass, Arnold; London, 1983
[96] Judith Brine, The Religious Intentions of the Cambridge Camden Society, 1991,.Fabrications: The Journal of the Society of Architectural Historians, Australia and New Zealand, vol 2, issue 1.
[97] Gerald Robinson, Experimenting with the Liturgy. 1993 Liturgy Canada vol iii No 2, The Hoskin Group, Toronto
[98] Tu aperuisti credentibus regna caelorum.

CHAPTER THIRTEEN
The Thirteenth Guest

In an Upper Room thirteen friends meet and have a meal together. During that meal Jesus takes a loaf of bread and after he has given thanks for it ("thanksgiving" in Greek is εύχαριστία, or eucharistia) he broke off pieces and gave them to his friends and followers, saying "This is my body. As often as you take it, remember me."

At that point one of the friends who had secretly betrayed Jesus to the authorities is burdened with so much guilt he feels he has to leave early, but before he goes Jesus makes sure that he too is fed. Judas Iscariot left an empty seat, and Jesus lets it remain empty. He did not choose who should make up the company, he left that choice open.

That seat is still empty, it has been empty down the centuries. The person to fill it could be anyone, could be an atheist, could be you or me. Many atheists have already accepted the invitation to continue Jesus' ministry of creating on earth a Kingdom of harmony, peace, fulfillment and justice. There is room at the table for more. Humanity is evolving: a new world is waiting to be born.

Index

A

Abelard, Peter, 27
agnostics, 151, 153
Alice in Wonderland, 29
Andrewes, Launcelot, 110
Anglicans, 132, 143, 146
Anselm (Saint), 27
Answers in Genesis, 51
Aristarchus, 44
atheists, 24, 33, 62, 100–102, 118, 142–144, 148, 159, 167
Auden W. H., 16
Augustine of Hippo, 7, 27

B

Barr, Stephen M., 4
belief, 5, 24, 27, 29, 32, 95, 131, 145, 147, 151, 153
believers, *See* people-of-faith
Bibby, Reginald, 145
Blind Watchmaker, The, 81
breath, 13
Brown, Laurence, 153
Bruno, Giordano, 44
Buddhism, 13
Byrne, Rhonda, 22

C

Calvin, John, 160
Cambridge Camden Soc., 161
CERN Collider, 56
Children of Peace, 96
Chögyam Trungpa, 24
Christ, 123, 165
Christianity 146, 122, 164
Christianity, 105, 106, 122, 123
church buildings, 161, 162
churches
    Holy Trinity/Toronto, 132–137
    Saint Jacques/Boucherie, 9
Churchill, Winston S., 53
clairvoyants, 84
Clarke, John, 5
Claudel, Paul, 10
Colonnade, The, 70
consciousness, universal, 14–18, 85
Copernicus. Nicolas, 44
Creation Museum, 48
Creationists, 47, 80

D

Darwin, Charles, 79
Dawkins, Richard, 39, 79, 102, 147
death, 10, 14, 35, 83
Denominations,
    Anglican, 53, 88, 132, 143,
    Christ Scientist, 25
    Episcopalian, 146–148
    Orthodox, 145
    Roman Catholic, 3, 4, 141, 147, 148
    Salvation Army, 99
    United Church, 138
    Unity Church, 20
Descartes, René, 17
design, 66, 67, 72, 75, 77, 78
dolphins, 41
doubt, 2, 36, 138, 154

E

Einstein, Albert, 3
Eliot, T. S., 76
Episcopalian, 53, 132, 146–148

Essenes, 109
Eratosthenes, 44
eternal life, 5, 6, 16, 85, 86
Evangelists, 18, 20
evolution, 41, 69, 71
Exodus, 42
Expo67, Montreal, 74

F

faith, 4, 27, 98, 123, 131
forgiveness, 121
Freemasonry, 46, 131
Funes, Rev. José G., 46

G

Galileo Galilei, 44
Genesis, 42, 56, 80
gods, 52, 76, 111
God, 7, 24, 42, 53, 62, 105, 153
gratitude, 135

H

Heavenly Father, 105, 111
Heisenberg, Werner, 4
Heloïse, 29
Hoffer, Eric, 70
Holy Trinity, 111

I

Ignatius (Saint), 140

J

Jansen, Cornelius, 7
Jenkins, Bishop David, 122
Jesus,
   his appearance, 106
   his attributes, 121–129
   his role, 144
   his son-ship, 105
   his teaching, 121
Josephus, Flavius, 106
Jung, Carl Gustav, 26, 131

K

Keats, John, 100
Krauss, Lawrence, 59

L

Large Hadron Collider, 56
Lederman, Leon M., 56

M

Mark Twain, 5, 89, 96, 105
miracles, 108–111
Mitchell, Alanna, 124
Muslim, 91, 96, 99

N

nervous system, 22, 74
New Thought movement, 16, 18
Newton, Isaac, 3, 4
non-existence, 3, 118

O

Osteen, Joel, 18, 24

P

Paley, William, 77
Pascal, Blaise, 5, 64, 100
Paul (Saint), 111
people of faith, 30, 39, 53, 63, 81, 141, 153, 159, 164
Phipps, Moderator Bill, 138
Piet Hein, 66

Planck, Max, 4
Ponder, Catherine, 20
Popes
    Clement VIII, 45
    Innocent X, 98
    John Paul II, 47
    Leo XIII, 46
    Paul VI, 51
    Pius X, 48, 108
prajna, 13
Ptolemy, 44

Q

Quakers, 96
Quantum Theory, 3, 54
Quimby, Phineas P., 16, 18, 25
Qumran, 109, 112

R

Ranjan Pilai, 67
Relativity, Theory of, 3, 54
Robbins, Tony, 20
Roman Catholic, 3, 4, 141, 148
Russell, Bertrand, 154

S

Sagan, Carl, 102, 135, 149
Sartre, Jean-Paul, 89
Schrödinger, Erwin, 155
Schuller, Robert H., 18
science, 2, 32, 101, 135
Science, Laws of, 3, 5, 101
Scutum Fidei, 113
Seasick, 124
Secret, The, 22
Shaw, George Bernard, 76, 82, 89, 147
Shiva Nataraja, 4, 62, 63
soul, the, 13
spirituality, 24

Stevens, Wallace, 112
Super Collider, The, 55

T

Tennessee Williams, 14
Terrorism, 98
Tertullian, 111
The Secret, 22
Torah, 42
Trinity College, Toronto, 5, 40, 58, 85, 137
Truths, provisional, 32, 100, 102, 112, 153
Truths, permanent, 32, 33, 34, 35, 51, 83, 87, 98, 100, 101, 102, 112, 137, 152
Twenty-Four Parts, 22, 23, 74

U

Unity Church, 20
universe, 7, 45, 53, 54, 57, 59, 80

V

vacuum, 8
Venetian Village, 72
virgin births, 108

W

Wattles, W. D., 20
Weil, Simone, 123
Williams, Robin, 146–148
Wren, Sir Christopher, 16

Y

Yahweh, 43

Z

zero, 7, 2, 29, 54, 57

Typeset in Palatino Linotype 11pt on 14pt. designed by Hermann Zapf, with headings in 12pt. Arial Black Italic. Illustrations drawn in Architrion 5.8. Printed in the USA.

www.ingramcontent.com/pod-product-compliance
Lightning Source LLC
Chambersburg PA
CBHW051101160426
43193CB00010B/1266